HELEN OF WYNDHORN™

And in between it all we'd stop and we'd drink and we'd laugh.
And it was all so wonderful.

HELEN OF WYNDHORN™

STORY BY
TOM KING

ART BY
BILQUIS EVELY

COLORS BY
MATHEUS LOPES

LETTERS BY
CLAYTON COWLES

COVER & CHAPTER BREAKS BY
BILQUIS EVELY
WITH MATHEUS LOPES

DARK HORSE BOOKS

PRESIDENT & PUBLISHER
MIKE RICHARDSON

EDITOR
DANIEL CHABON

ASSISTING EDITOR
CHUCK HOWITT-LEASE

ASSISTANT EDITOR
MISHA GEHR

DESIGNER
HANNAH NOBLE

DIGITAL ART TECHNICIAN
ADAM PRUETT

Helen of Wyndhorn

Collects *Helen of Wyndhorn* #1–#6.

Published by **Dark Horse Books**
A division of Dark Horse Comics LLC
10956 SE Main Street
Milwaukie, OR 97222

DarkHorse.com

Represented in the EU by Authorised Rep Compliance Ltd.
Ground Floor, 71 Lower Baggot Street
Dublin, D02 P593, Ireland
ARCCompliance.com

To find a comics shop in your area, visit **comicshoplocator.com**

First edition: February 2025

Ebook ISBN 978-1-50674-008-9
Hardcover ISBN 978-1-50674-006-5

3 5 7 9 10 8 6 4

MIX
Paper | Supporting responsible forestry
FSC® C169962
FSC www.fsc.org

Printed in China

Bilquis Evely '23
Mat Lopes

CHAPTER I

I didn't know him.
The father, yes.
And the daughter.
Helen.

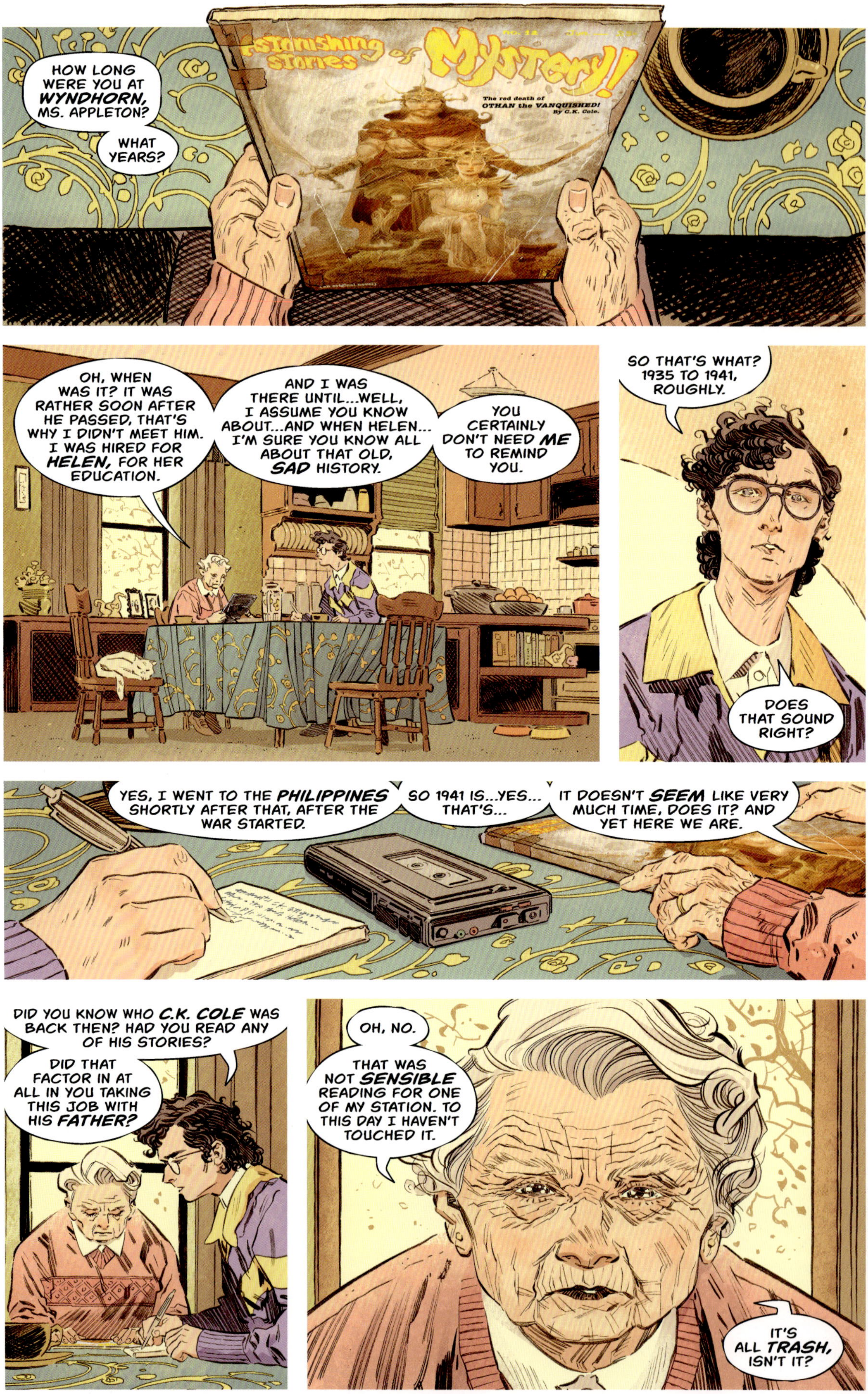

Astonishing Stories of Mystery!
The red death of OTHAN the VANQUISHED! By C.K. Cole.
HOW LONG WERE YOU AT WYNDHORN, MS. APPLETON?
WHAT YEARS?
OH, WHEN WAS IT? IT WAS RATHER SOON AFTER HE PASSED, THAT'S WHY I DIDN'T MEET HIM. I WAS HIRED FOR HELEN, FOR HER EDUCATION.
AND I WAS THERE UNTIL...WELL, I ASSUME YOU KNOW ABOUT...AND WHEN HELEN... I'M SURE YOU KNOW ALL ABOUT THAT OLD, SAD HISTORY.
YOU CERTAINLY DON'T NEED ME TO REMIND YOU.
SO THAT'S WHAT? 1935 TO 1941, ROUGHLY.
DOES THAT SOUND RIGHT?
YES, I WENT TO THE PHILIPPINES SHORTLY AFTER THAT, AFTER THE WAR STARTED.
SO 1941 IS...YES... THAT'S...
IT DOESN'T SEEM LIKE VERY MUCH TIME, DOES IT? AND YET HERE WE ARE.
DID YOU KNOW WHO C.K. COLE WAS BACK THEN? HAD YOU READ ANY OF HIS STORIES?
DID THAT FACTOR IN AT ALL IN YOU TAKING THIS JOB WITH HIS FATHER?
OH, NO.
THAT WAS NOT SENSIBLE READING FOR ONE OF MY STATION. TO THIS DAY I HAVEN'T TOUCHED IT.
IT'S ALL TRASH, ISN'T IT?

All I knew is that a great man had hired me as a governess for his poor granddaughter, who had recently been orphaned.
And my first task was to travel down to Texas and fetch the young lady back to the man's manor.
I had been given the address of a small inn near the town of San Antonio where I was to meet her.
And I proceeded there with appropriate haste.
However, upon reaching the establishment, which was more motel than inn, I was informed that she had been removed from the premises for not paying her bill.
Though they had little notion where she might then be living, they recommended I seek her at a local tavern she often frequented.
I thought this rather preposterous. This was a girl of only sixteen, after all.
But with no other recourse, I followed the man's advice, and to my shock, the proprietors of that taproom did indeed know the young lady.
In truth, merely the mention of her name provoked unconstrained and rather rude giggles from the barkeep.
It has been over five decades and still I hesitate to admit where he sent me next.
Needless to say, it was my first visit to such an establishment.
And though I found the constables friendly and patient, the desperation of the incarcerated was unmistakably in the air all around me.
I would not again suffer such smells and noises until I nursed at a hospital in the Far East.

And that is where I first encountered Miss Helen Cole.
HELEN, WAKE UP! YOU GOT A VISITOR!
WHAT?
STOP IT.
MISS COLE, IT IS A PLEASURE TO MAKE YOUR ACQUAINTANCE. MY NAME IS LILITH APPLETON. I AM A GOVERNESS IN THE EMPLOY OF YOUR GRANDFATHER.
FIRST, ALLOW ME TO EXPRESS MY DEEPEST SYMPATHY FOR THE RECENT LOSS OF YOUR FATHER.
SECOND, I AM PLEASED TO SAY, I HAVE BEEN SENT HERE TO ACCOMPANY YOU ON YOUR TRIP BACK TO WYNDHORN HOUSE.
NNNN.

After some negotiation, I was able to secure Helen's freedom by making a few reasonable donations to various police causes.
THE TRAIN IS LEAVING IN FOUR HOURS, WHICH GIVES US PLENTY OF TIME TO GET TO THE STATION.
HOW MUCH MONEY DO YOU HAVE, LILITH?
Attempting to secure the girl's trust and not yet knowing the extent of her habits, I went along with her suggestion of where to spend the afternoon.
SHOT AND CHASER FOR ME, HANK! LILITH, WHAT DO YOU WANT?
WATER. IN A CLEAN GLASS.
WATER IN A CLEAN GLASS FOR LILITH!
AND A PACK OF CHESTERTONS! DON'T WORRY, SHE'S GOT PLENTY OF DOUGH!
ARE YOU NOT A TOUCH YOUNG?
HAHAHA.
WHERE WERE YOU WHEN I WAS ELEVEN?
YOU WERE NOT THEN IN MY CARE, AS YOU NOW ARE.
WE GOT TO MAKE ANOTHER STOP.
DON'T DAWDLE WITH THAT WATER NOW, LILITH APPLETON.

After more rounds of drinks than I would have expected from the most experienced of lushes, we proceeded to walk a few blocks east.
To the shop of a stone sculptor.
OKAY, YEAH, THIS ONE'S GOOD.
YOU DO THE WRITING TOO?
YES, MA'AM. ENGRAVING IS A DOLLAR A LETTER.
WELL, I WANT, LIKE, BIG LETTERS THAT SAY:
"CHRISTOPHER KRIEGER COLE, 1900–1935."
AND THEN BELOW IT, JUST... "BETTER THAN SHAKESPEARE."
YOU GOT THAT?
I'M LEAVING TOWN, BUT I TOLD DADDY I'D COME BACK EACH YEAR AND VISIT.
SO BY THE TIME I'M BACK HERE, I DON'T WANT TO SEE THAT WOODEN CROSS WE GOT THERE.
WE'RE GOING TO PAY GOOD MONEY, I BETTER SEE IT ALL LOOKING GOOD, ALL RIGHT?
IT'LL BE NICE, ALL SET UP BY THEN, FOR SURE. ON MY WORD.
BUT HOW IS IT YOU'RE SPELLING THAT "SHAKESPEARE" THERE, MA'AM?
HOW THE HELL WOULD I KNOW?
LOOK IT UP IN A BOOK.

I MEAN, I'VE ACTUALLY BEEN TO THAT GRAVE. THERE *IS* AN ANGEL.
YOU KNOW THERE'S A LOT OF ARGUMENTS BETWEEN SCHOLARS OVER WHAT THE INSCRIPTION MEANS, *IF* IT EXPLAINS ANYTHING.
PEOPLE HAVE *PUBLISHED* ON THE SUBJECT. IT'S FASCINATING.
THE GENERAL CONSENSUS SEEMS TO BE THAT THEY WERE HIS LAST WORDS BEFORE HE KILLED HIMSELF, THAT HE DICTATED THEM.
I DON'T THINK *ANYONE'S* YET ATTRIBUTED IT TO HELEN.
WELL, *I* HELPED HER SPELL IT.
DO *YOU* KNOW WHAT IT MEANS?
HM.
I LEARNED.

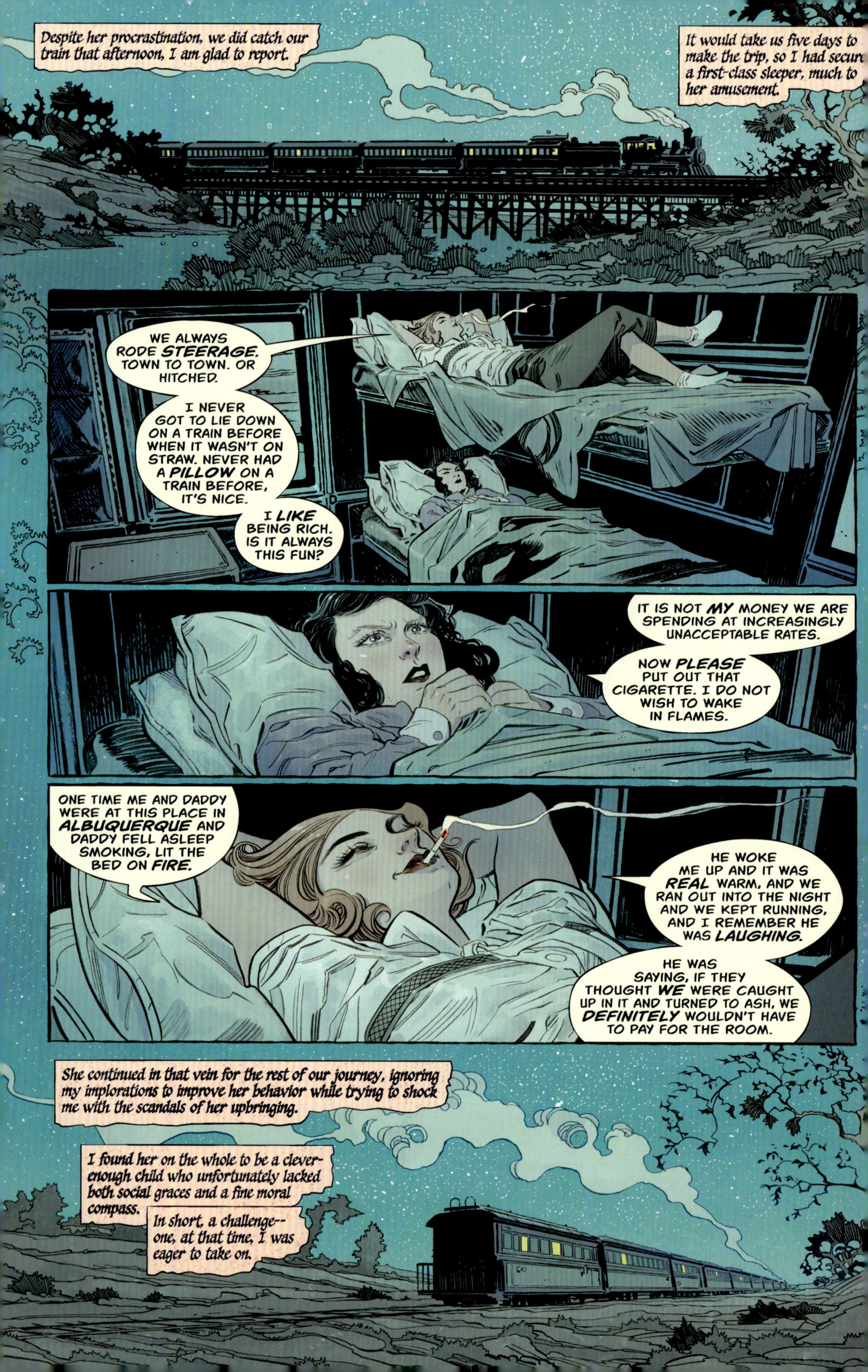
Despite her procrastination, we did catch our train that afternoon, I am glad to report.
It would take us five days to make the trip, so I had secur a first-class sleeper, much to her amusement.
WE ALWAYS RODE STEERAGE. TOWN TO TOWN. OR HITCHED.
I NEVER GOT TO LIE DOWN ON A TRAIN BEFORE WHEN IT WASN'T ON STRAW. NEVER HAD A PILLOW ON A TRAIN BEFORE, IT'S NICE.
I LIKE BEING RICH. IS IT ALWAYS THIS FUN?
IT IS NOT MY MONEY WE ARE SPENDING AT INCREASINGLY UNACCEPTABLE RATES.
NOW PLEASE PUT OUT THAT CIGARETTE. I DO NOT WISH TO WAKE IN FLAMES.
ONE TIME ME AND DADDY WERE AT THIS PLACE IN ALBUQUERQUE AND DADDY FELL ASLEEP SMOKING, LIT THE BED ON FIRE.
HE WOKE ME UP AND IT WAS REAL WARM, AND WE RAN OUT INTO THE NIGHT AND WE KEPT RUNNING, AND I REMEMBER HE WAS LAUGHING.
HE WAS SAYING, IF THEY THOUGHT WE WERE CAUGHT UP IN IT AND TURNED TO ASH, WE DEFINITELY WOULDN'T HAVE TO PAY FOR THE ROOM.
She continued in that vein for the rest of our journey, ignoring my implorations to improve her behavior while trying to shock me with the scandals of her upbringing.
I found her on the whole to be a clever-enough child who unfortunately lacked both social graces and a fine moral compass.
In short, a challenge--one, at that time, I was eager to take on.

Finally, our travel ended.
And we reached dear **Wyndhorn**.

Joseph, the head (and only) butler of the house, met us at the station and drove us out to the property.
I had met Joseph earlier when I had interviewed for my position, and I cannot say I cared for him then or ever learned to thereafter.
He was a cold man whose attempts to hide his constant judgments were in fact projections of those very opinions.
MADAMS.
As I abhor gossip, I of course kept my impressions of the man to myself and let my charge develop her own.
WYNDHORN HOUSE CONTAINS 173 COMELY ROOMS AND IS SITUATED ON 1,200 ACRES OF FERTILE LAND.
IT IS INDEED VERY MUCH IN THE CHARACTER OF YOUR LATE FATHER TO DESCRIBE THAT ACCOMPLISHMENT AS MERELY "BIG."
DAD SAID HE WAS RAISED IN A BIG HOUSE.
I THOUGHT HE MEANT MAYBE TWO ROOMS. INDOOR TOILET.
YOU KNEW HIM?
I WITNESSED HIS BIRTH AND UPBRINGING.
WHETHER I KNEW HIM, I LEAVE THAT CONCLUSION TO WISER GODS THAN I.

By that point in my life I had worked in several fine homes of the best reputation, manors built and decorated to impress the highest of nobility.
MISS HELEN COLE.
IT IS MY HONOR TO WELCOME YOU HOME.
And even I had to concede that Wyndhorn soared above them all.
JESUS FUCKING CHRIST.
THE MASTER, REGRETFULLY, HAS BEEN CALLED AWAY AT THE MOMENT. HE WILL BE RETURNING AT THE END OF THE MONTH.
HOWEVER, I HAVE BEEN INSTRUCTED TO GIVE YOU A TOUR OF THE ROOMS. WE MAY DO THAT NOW OR AFTER YOU HAVE RESTED.
THE CHOICE IS YOURS.
I WANT TO SEE IT ALL.

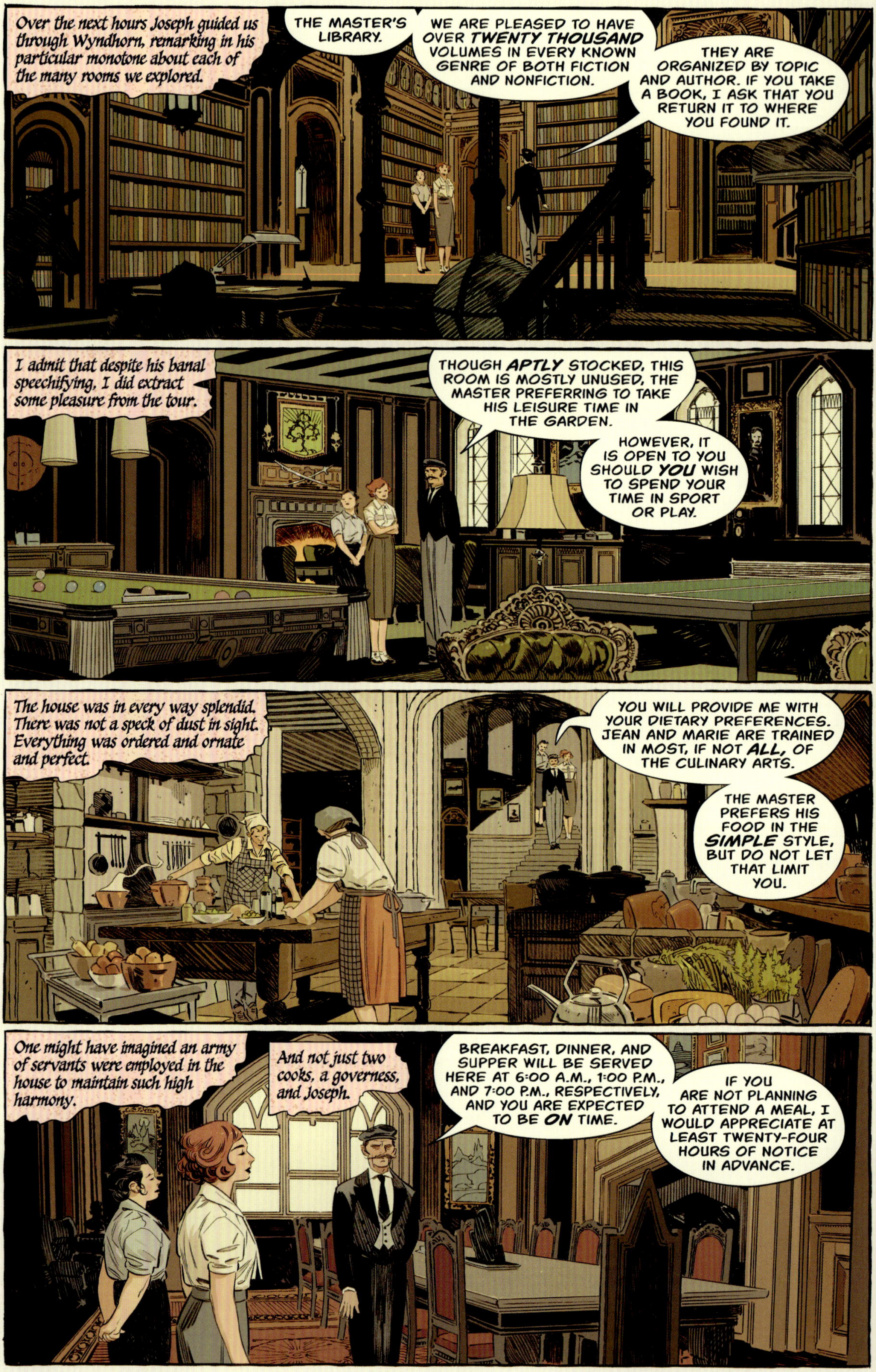
Over the next hours Joseph guided us through Wyndhorn, remarking in his particular monotone about each of the many rooms we explored.
THE MASTER'S LIBRARY.
WE ARE PLEASED TO HAVE OVER TWENTY THOUSAND VOLUMES IN EVERY KNOWN GENRE OF BOTH FICTION AND NONFICTION.
THEY ARE ORGANIZED BY TOPIC AND AUTHOR. IF YOU TAKE A BOOK, I ASK THAT YOU RETURN IT TO WHERE YOU FOUND IT.
I admit that despite his banal speechifying, I did extract some pleasure from the tour.
THOUGH APTLY STOCKED, THIS ROOM IS MOSTLY UNUSED, THE MASTER PREFERRING TO TAKE HIS LEISURE TIME IN THE GARDEN.
HOWEVER, IT IS OPEN TO YOU SHOULD YOU WISH TO SPEND YOUR TIME IN SPORT OR PLAY.
The house was in every way splendid. There was not a speck of dust in sight. Everything was ordered and ornate and perfect.
YOU WILL PROVIDE ME WITH YOUR DIETARY PREFERENCES. JEAN AND MARIE ARE TRAINED IN MOST, IF NOT ALL, OF THE CULINARY ARTS.
THE MASTER PREFERS HIS FOOD IN THE SIMPLE STYLE, BUT DO NOT LET THAT LIMIT YOU.
One might have imagined an army of servants were employed in the house to maintain such high harmony.
And not just two cooks, a governess, and Joseph.
BREAKFAST, DINNER, AND SUPPER WILL BE SERVED HERE AT 6:00 A.M., 1:00 P.M., AND 7:00 P.M., RESPECTIVELY, AND YOU ARE EXPECTED TO BE ON TIME.
IF YOU ARE NOT PLANNING TO ATTEND A MEAL, I WOULD APPRECIATE AT LEAST TWENTY-FOUR HOURS OF NOTICE IN ADVANCE.

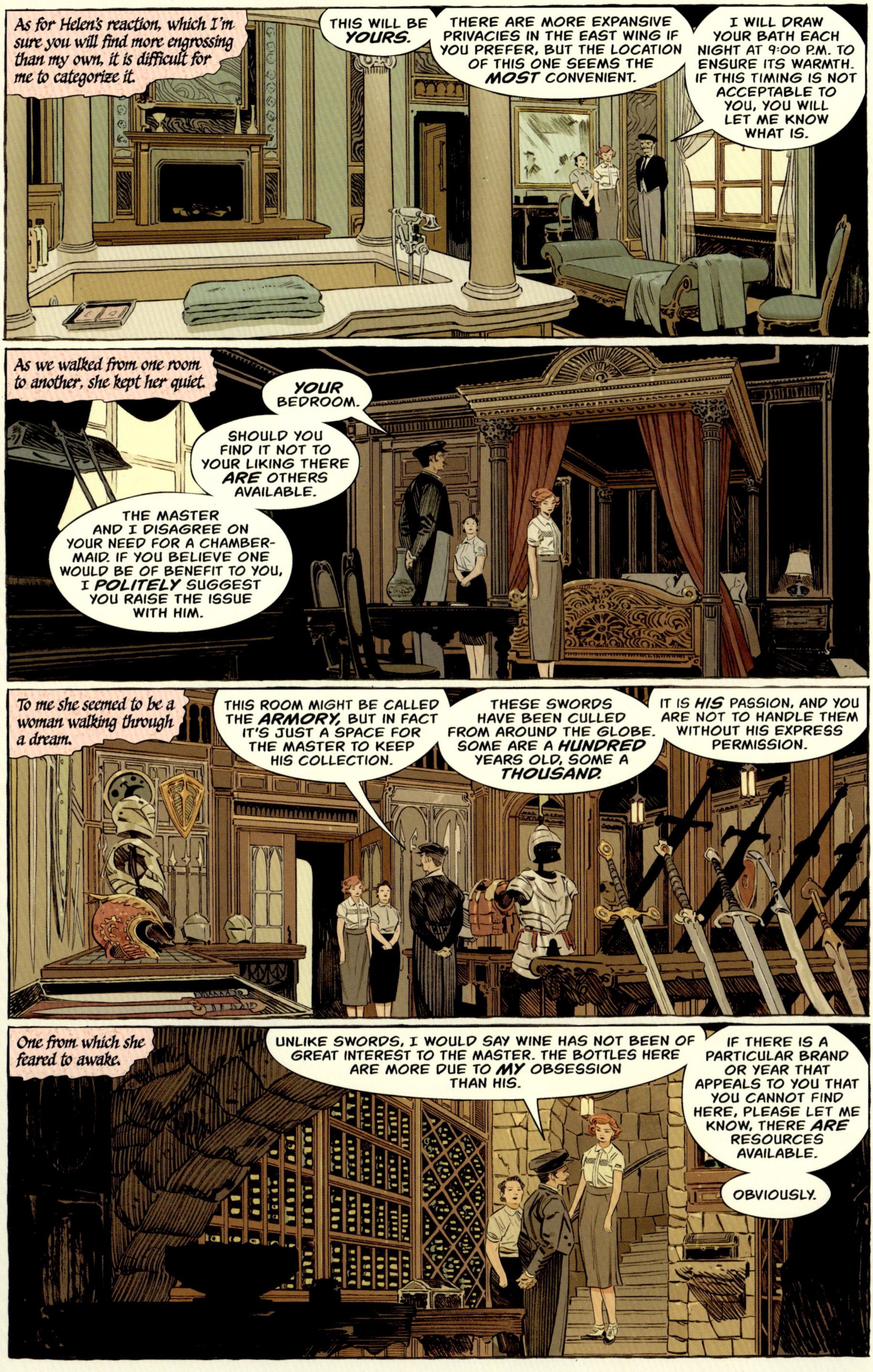
As for Helen's reaction, which I'm sure you will find more engrossing than my own, it is difficult for me to categorize it.
THIS WILL BE YOURS.
THERE ARE MORE EXPANSIVE PRIVACIES IN THE EAST WING IF YOU PREFER, BUT THE LOCATION OF THIS ONE SEEMS THE MOST CONVENIENT.
I WILL DRAW YOUR BATH EACH NIGHT AT 9:00 P.M. TO ENSURE ITS WARMTH. IF THIS TIMING IS NOT ACCEPTABLE TO YOU, YOU WILL LET ME KNOW WHAT IS.
As we walked from one room to another, she kept her quiet.
YOUR BEDROOM.
SHOULD YOU FIND IT NOT TO YOUR LIKING THERE ARE OTHERS AVAILABLE.
THE MASTER AND I DISAGREE ON YOUR NEED FOR A CHAMBER-MAID. IF YOU BELIEVE ONE WOULD BE OF BENEFIT TO YOU, I POLITELY SUGGEST YOU RAISE THE ISSUE WITH HIM.
To me she seemed to be a woman walking through a dream.
THIS ROOM MIGHT BE CALLED THE ARMORY, BUT IN FACT IT'S JUST A SPACE FOR THE MASTER TO KEEP HIS COLLECTION.
THESE SWORDS HAVE BEEN CULLED FROM AROUND THE GLOBE. SOME ARE A HUNDRED YEARS OLD, SOME A THOUSAND.
IT IS HIS PASSION, AND YOU ARE NOT TO HANDLE THEM WITHOUT HIS EXPRESS PERMISSION.
One from which she feared to awake.
UNLIKE SWORDS, I WOULD SAY WINE HAS NOT BEEN OF GREAT INTEREST TO THE MASTER. THE BOTTLES HERE ARE MORE DUE TO MY OBSESSION THAN HIS.
IF THERE IS A PARTICULAR BRAND OR YEAR THAT APPEALS TO YOU THAT YOU CANNOT FIND HERE, PLEASE LET ME KNOW, THERE ARE RESOURCES AVAILABLE.
OBVIOUSLY.

Eventually, though, her silence broke.
ALSO IF YOU HAVE A QUESTION ABOUT A SPECIFIC VINTAGE, I'D BE HAPPY TO TELL YOU THE HISTORY OF BOTH ITS MAKE AND ACQUISITION.
THIS IS GOOD.
AH, I SEE YOU HAVE FOUND THE NAPOLEON ROUGE 1857, AN EXCELLENT CHOICE. IT WAS QUITE AN ORDEAL TO ACQUIRE, I DON'T MIND--
THANK YOU.
GKRAKKK
EXCUSE ME...YOUNG LADY...
I COULD... THAT...AT LEAST ALLOW ME TO DECANT IT FOR YOU SO YOU MIGHT...
...ENJOY IT TO ITS...FULL... POTENTIAL...
MISS COLE!
THIS IS NOT PROPER!
I'M DONE WITH THE TOUR.
I'M JUST GOING TO GO BACK THERE NOW.
IT'S A SWELL HOUSE. THANK YOU.

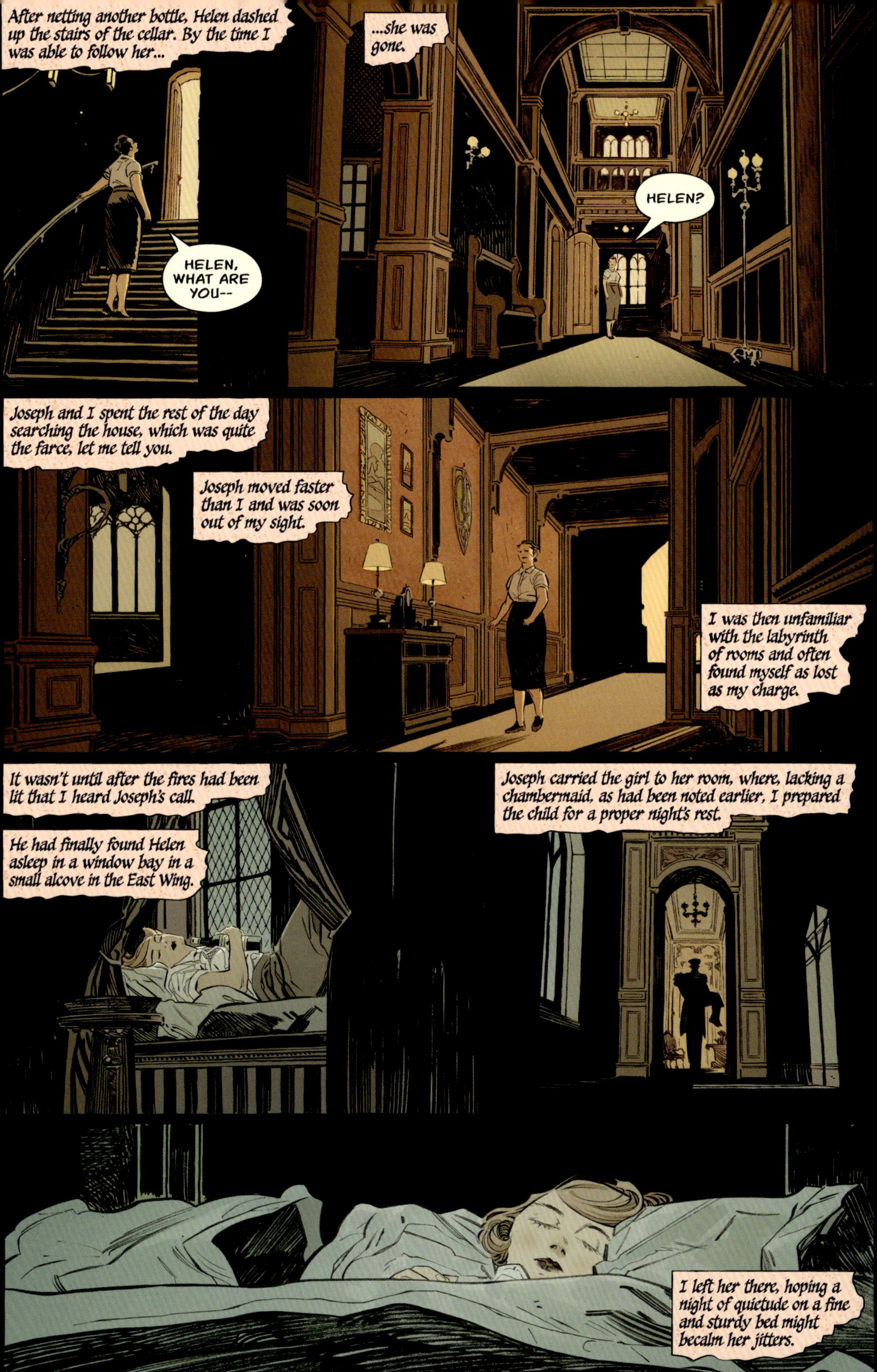
After netting another bottle, Helen dashed up the stairs of the cellar. By the time I was able to follow her...
HELEN, WHAT ARE YOU--
...she was gone.
HELEN?
Joseph and I spent the rest of the day searching the house, which was quite the farce, let me tell you.
Joseph moved faster than I and was soon out of my sight.
I was then unfamiliar with the labyrinth of rooms and often found myself as lost as my charge.
It wasn't until after the fires had been lit that I heard Joseph's call.
He had finally found Helen asleep in a window bay in a small alcove in the East Wing.
Joseph carried the girl to her room, where, lacking a chambermaid, as had been noted earlier, I prepared the child for a proper night's rest.
I left her there, hoping a night of quietude on a fine and sturdy bed might becalm her jitters.

I retired that night to my own room in the servants' wing. Though there were more lavish accommodations in Wyndhorn, I insisted on something modest.
I believe thoroughly in living within one's place and means.
I slept soundly and it must have been past two in the morning when I was shocked awake by the sound of Helen's voice.
LILITH.
How she found my room that night, I do not know. Perhaps in her explorations earlier in the day she had come across it.
CAN I STAY WITH YOU? I'M SORRY, THERE WAS A NOISE, AND I WOKE UP.
I LOOKED OUT MY WINDOW.
Perhaps other, stranger forces were at play in that late hour.
THERE WAS A MONSTER THERE.
However it had come about was not my concern at the moment. The girl looked a fright and held my sympathies.
ALL RIGHT, DEAR, COME, COME.
IT'S GOING TO BE FINE. NIGHTMARES ARE AS NATURAL AS RAIN.
And that was how Helen spent her first night in her new home.

This pattern, I am loath but obligated to report, continued unabated over the next few weeks.
Though I attempted to begin our lessons, Helen spent every minute of her day avoiding Joseph and me.
Until we'd find her in some room or another, her eyes closed, her breath deep, a bottle clutched to her bosom.
Inevitably, we'd bring her to her room.
And, inevitably, in the middle of the night, she'd be back in my bed, rambling on about the imagined horrors out her window.
Before you ask, we of course locked the cellar door in the hopes of curtailing her unusual consumption.
However, by the time that had been accomplished she had absconded with dozens of bottles, which were then well hid throughout the property.
She was indeed a clever girl.
When not searching for the young lady, Joseph and I spent our time debating what to do.
WE MIGHT CHAIN HER.
AND HAVE YOU CHAINS, JOSEPH?
These sessions were less than productive.
I DO.
BUT THEY MAY BE TOO LARGE FOR THIS TASK.
And days and nights passed with, I am sorry to say, very little improvement.
As the end of the month neared, we knew very well that the master of the house was to return shortly.
We were distressed over his certain fury at our inability to have any control over his ward.

I NEED CIGARETTES.
SMOKING IS A FILTHY FASHION USED BY SINNERS TO DISTRACT FROM THEIR NEEDS FOR PENANCE.
I DO NOT CONDONE IT, AND I WILL CERTAINLY NOT AID IN IT.
JOSEPH SAYS THE TOWN IS THREE HUNDRED MILES AWAY. I DON'T DRIVE.
HE WON'T TAKE ME.
THIS IS HOW YOU WISH TO SPEND YOUR LIFE?
WILD, SOUSED, AND DESPERATE?
IT'S HOW MY FATHER SPENT HIS, AND HE WAS THE GREATEST WRITER OF HIS GENERATION.
WOULD YOU LIKE IT BETTER IF HE LIVED IT LIKE YOU? SMALL AND FORGOTTEN?
YOUR FATHER IS DEAD.
AS FOR HIS REPUTATION.
I AM UNFAMILIAR WITH HIS OEUVRE, BUT MY UNDERSTANDING IS THAT IT WAS NOT EXACTLY SUNG IN THE HALLS OF THE ACADEMY.

I NEED CIGARETTES!
NO, MY DEAR.
YOU NEED DISCIPLINE.
QUITE A BIT OF IT, IN FACT.
MY FATHER ESCAPED! MY FATHER WAS FREE!
CRAKSHH
LET THE ACADEMY FUCKING SING THAT!
We found her later of course wrapped in a ball, an empty bottle in her arms, like a child might hold on to a stuffed bear.
The situation was steadily evolving from worrisome to tiresome.
TSK TSK TSK.

All the greater then was my shock when I was awakened that night not by the soft fall of her guilty footsteps.
But by her shriek of terror somewhere outside my window.
AAAAH!
HELEN?
I grabbed a small gas lamp I kept by my bed and sped toward the screams.
As I went I called out for Joseph's help.
JOSEPH! JOSEPH!
But received no answer.
With no other option available, I exited the house alone in search of Helen.
By that time her cries filled the air and visions of her at the mercy of robbers or wolves spilled into my imagination.
AAAAAH!
Some thirty feet from the entrance to Wyndhorn I spied the girl running toward me in a panic.
LILITH!
IT'S HERE!
I was by this time accustomed to her night terrors and assumed this occasion to be no more than another fantasia of fright.
HUSH, CHILD! YOU HAVE WORKED YOURSELF INTO A STATE.
ALL THAT IS OUT AT THIS HOUR ARE THE OWLS AND THE--
JESUS CHRIST...JESUS CHRIST...
This, then, is when I heard its roar.
--MOON.
I'M...I'M SORRY, I'M REALLY SORRY...
ROARRRR!

I am not C.K. Cole, and I will not attempt its description as he undoubtedly would. All that fang-and-blood vocabulary.
I will simply say out of the dark came a monster, and I feared greatly for my life and that of the child.
RAAURRR!
My first reaction was simply to scream.
I wish I were made of more brave stock, and I feel if you look at the totality of my life you might find that I am.
AAAAAAH!
GRARRR!
But at that particular moment, with that singularly wicked thing charging toward us, intent no doubt to tear into our flesh, I found myself all but paralyzed.
That I had enough breath to call out into the dark is a minor miracle in and of itself.
And though I do not take pride in my panic, I am grateful that within that flash of pure dread, at least something was done.

URGH!
But just as it was upon us, just as I could feel its hell-born breath charring my cheek, it seemed to rear back in a jolt of pain.
It turned away from us, its prey, and peered frantically back into the black of the woods and the fields.
As if it was being called.
Then, to my everlasting relief, with the same alacrity with which it had attacked us, it launched itself in the opposite direction.
Though I shamefully had neither the time nor instinct for prayer in the moment of my certain death, I do believe God saw me all the same.
And granted us a respite.
Helen was at that moment weeping into my shoulder and so did not witness what I did that night as I forced my trembling eyes wide to confirm the monster's flight.
She did not see the sword blaze out of the darkness.
Nor the hand reaching for the bloody head.

No, by the time she had courage enough to turn away from my damp garment, all Helen saw was her grandfather.
Barnabas Cole.
Finally returned.

I'M SORRY, I DON'T THINK I UNDERSTAND.
UHM.
LIKE, THESE MONSTERS AND, UHM... WAS THIS, LIKE, A FANTASY? HELEN WAS HAVING PROBLEMS, LIKE A NIGHTMARE OR SOMETHING?
PROBLEMS WITH HER FATHER'S SUICIDE? LIKE MAYBE IT WAS THE SAME THING THAT HAUNTED HER FATHER, GIVEN THEIR SIMILAR FATES.
IS THIS...IS THAT IT? I DON'T GET IT.
NO.
I'M SORRY, THOMAS.
IT WAS NOT FANTASY.
IT WAS WYNDHORN.
AND IT WAS HELEN AND IT WAS BARNABAS AND IT WAS A MONSTER.
AND IT WAS JUST THE BEGINNING.

Bilquis Evely 23
Mat Lopes

CHAPTER
II

I REALLY ENJOYED THE BOOK, THANK YOU. THE ORIGINAL OTHAN BY COLE IS, LIKE, SO GOOD.
YOU KNOW, I THINK YOU ACTUALLY INTERVIEWED MY AUNT ABOUT IT.
LILITH APPLETON.
MY COUSIN SAID YOU, LIKE, INTERVIEWED HER OR SOMETHING 'CAUSE SHE WORKED FOR COLE IN THE '30s.
WHICH IS COOL. I DIDN'T EVEN KNOW.
SHE NEVER TALKED ABOUT IT.

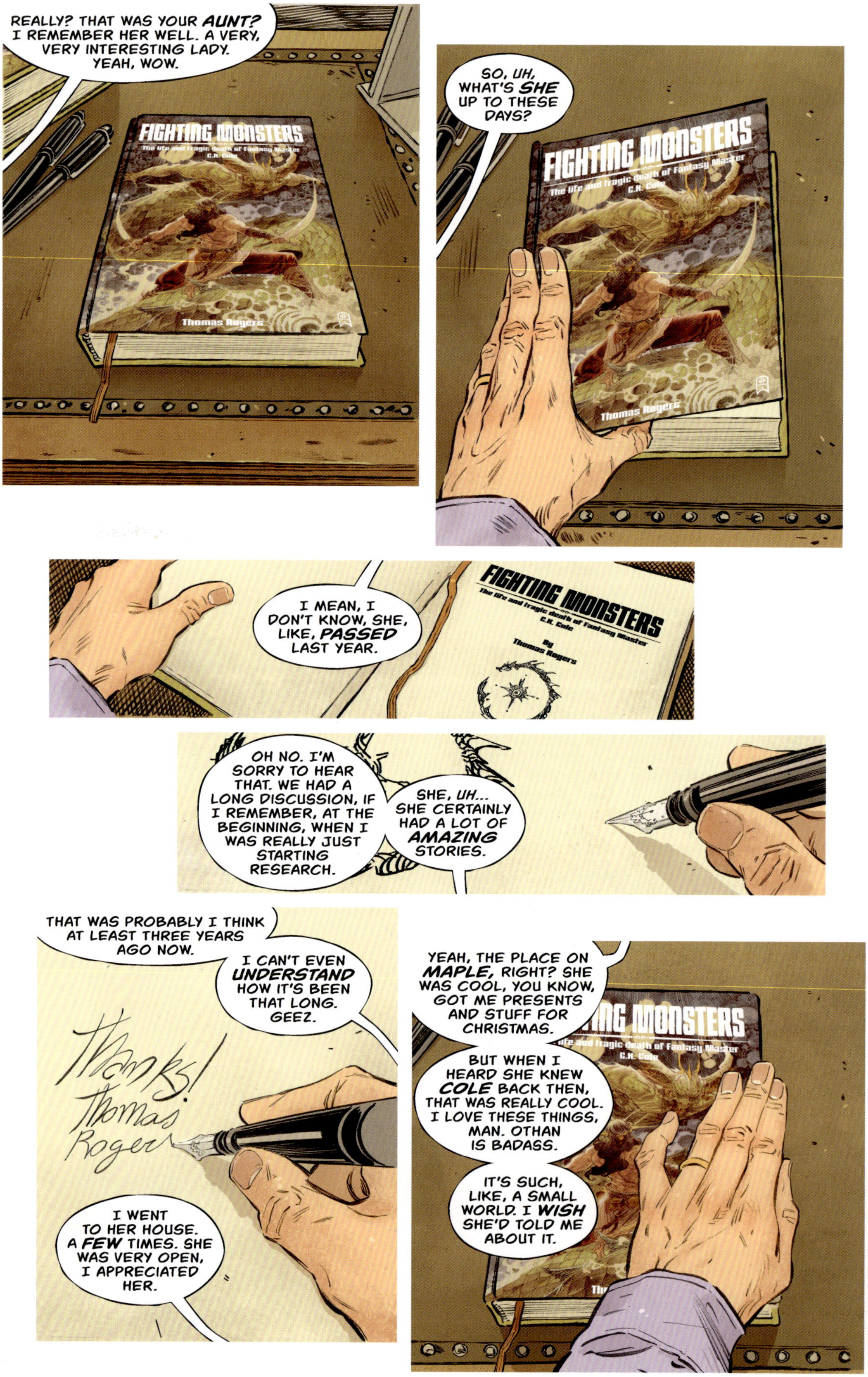
REALLY? THAT WAS YOUR AUNT? I REMEMBER HER WELL. A VERY, VERY INTERESTING LADY. YEAH, WOW.
FIGHTING MONSTERS
The life and tragic death of Fantasy Master
C.K. Cole
Thomas Rogers
SO, UH, WHAT'S SHE UP TO THESE DAYS?
I MEAN, I DON'T KNOW, SHE, LIKE, PASSED LAST YEAR.
FIGHTING MONSTERS
The life and tragic death of Fantasy Master
C.K. Cole
By
Thomas Rogers
OH NO. I'M SORRY TO HEAR THAT. WE HAD A LONG DISCUSSION, IF I REMEMBER, AT THE BEGINNING, WHEN I WAS REALLY JUST STARTING RESEARCH.
SHE, UH... SHE CERTAINLY HAD A LOT OF AMAZING STORIES.
THAT WAS PROBABLY I THINK AT LEAST THREE YEARS AGO NOW.
I CAN'T EVEN UNDERSTAND HOW IT'S BEEN THAT LONG. GEEZ.
Thanks! Thomas Rogers
I WENT TO HER HOUSE. A FEW TIMES. SHE WAS VERY OPEN, I APPRECIATED HER.
YEAH, THE PLACE ON MAPLE, RIGHT? SHE WAS COOL, YOU KNOW, GOT ME PRESENTS AND STUFF FOR CHRISTMAS.
BUT WHEN I HEARD SHE KNEW COLE BACK THEN, THAT WAS REALLY COOL. I LOVE THESE THINGS, MAN. OTHAN IS BADASS.
IT'S SUCH, LIKE, A SMALL WORLD. I WISH SHE'D TOLD ME ABOUT IT.

THE SOUP IS VERY PLEASANT.
MARIE HAS A MASTERY OF BROTH YOU DO NOT OFTEN FIND ON THIS SIDE OF THE ATLANTIC.
IT'S EXCELLENT.
MM.
EXCUSE ME...
...WHAT THE HELL IS HAPPENING?

After Barnabas slayed the monster in the dark, he slunk away without a word, leaving Helen and me in a state of shock.
HELEN, PLEASE, YOU WILL CONTROL YOUR MOUTH AROUND YOUR GRANDFATHER.
THIS IS A HOUSE OF GRACE. THERE IS NO PLACE HERE FOR SUCH COARSE LANGUAGE.
Helen made a valiant attempt to follow her grandfather, but the exhaustion of a danger passed had settled in her, and I was easily able to pull her back.
GRACE?
NO.
I helped her to the house, and she spent the night in my company, barely uttering a word.
WHAT WAS THAT?!
THAT THING?!
AND WHAT THE HELL DID YOU DO WITH IT?!
The next morning, she kept up her reserve, and surprisingly, kept by my side, avoiding her usual appetite for wine and respite.
HELEN, YOU WILL SIT DOWN.
THERE IS A TIME AND PLACE FOR CURIOSITY, AND THERE IS A TIME AND PLACE FOR MANNERS.
THIS IS YOUR GRANDFATHER'S TABLE.
We did not see the master all day. Joseph said he was out at the hunt.
WHO CARES WHOSE TABLE IT IS?!
GRACE? HEH.
Finally at dinner, Barnabas made his appearance, which in turn pried Helen from her seeming trap of silence.
SOMEONE HAS TO SAY WHAT THIS IS!
BANG

HEH.
NO.
LIKE THIS.
AAAAAAAH!
CKKRAAKK
And with nothing more than that, Barnabas left the meal.
And Joseph began to pick up the mess.

We did not see Barnabas for the rest of the evening.
Helen did not make even a pretense about staying in her own room that night.
I DON'T SEE ANYTHING.
MAYBE THEY HIDE FROM THE RAIN.
MAYBE HE KILLED THEM ALL.
MAYBE YOU ARE YOUNG AND DO NOT UNDERSTAND WHAT YOU THINK YOU OBSERVED.
WELL, YOU'RE OLD. WHAT DID YOU OBSERVE?
IN TERMS OF AGE, I HAVE BUT A FEW YEARS ON YOUR OWN, YOUNG MISS.
HOWEVER, IN TERMS OF MATURITY, I CAN UNDERSTAND YOUR MISCONCEPTION.
AND I BELIEVE A GOOD MAN SAVED US FROM A BAD WOLF. OR SOMETHING SIMILAR. SOMETHING EXOTIC, CERTAINLY, BUT NOTHING DISCONCERTING.
JESUS, LILITH.
I DON'T KNOW WHAT THE HELL YOU ARE.
BUT I'M ENTIRELY DISCONCERTED.

SIGH THE BEST THING FOR YOU IS TO FOCUS NOW ON YOUR EDUCATION.
WITH AN UNDERSTANDING OF MATHS AND THE LANGUAGE ARTS, YOU WILL COME TO AN--
KNOCK KNOCK
AT THIS HOUR?
REALLY. IS NOTHING VALUED IN THIS HOUSE?
JOSEPH, WE ARE QUITE SETTLED AND DO NOT REQUIRE--
THE MASTER OBLIGATED ME TO SEE THAT MISS COLE RECEIVE A PACKAGE OF CIGARETTES.
I WAS TOLD NOT TO WAIT UNTIL MORNING AND TO DELIVER THEM TO HER PERSONALLY.
THANK YOU, JOSEPH.
BUT YOUR QUEST IS AT AN END.
I WILL CARRY THE BURDEN THE REST OF THE WAY.
THAT IS NOT--
CIGARETTES? IN THE MIDDLE OF THE NIGHT? I NEVER.
I WOULDN'T BE SURPRISED IF THAT WASN'T OLD JOSEPH TRYING TO GET A GLANCE BEHIND A CURTAIN THAT HAS BEEN WELL DRAWN.
SOMETHING ELSE ON WHICH, REGRETTABLY, YOU MUST BE EDUCATED.
DON'T YOU SEE?
GRANDFATHER KNOWS WHY I LEFT.
NOW HE WANTS TO KEEP ME INSIDE.

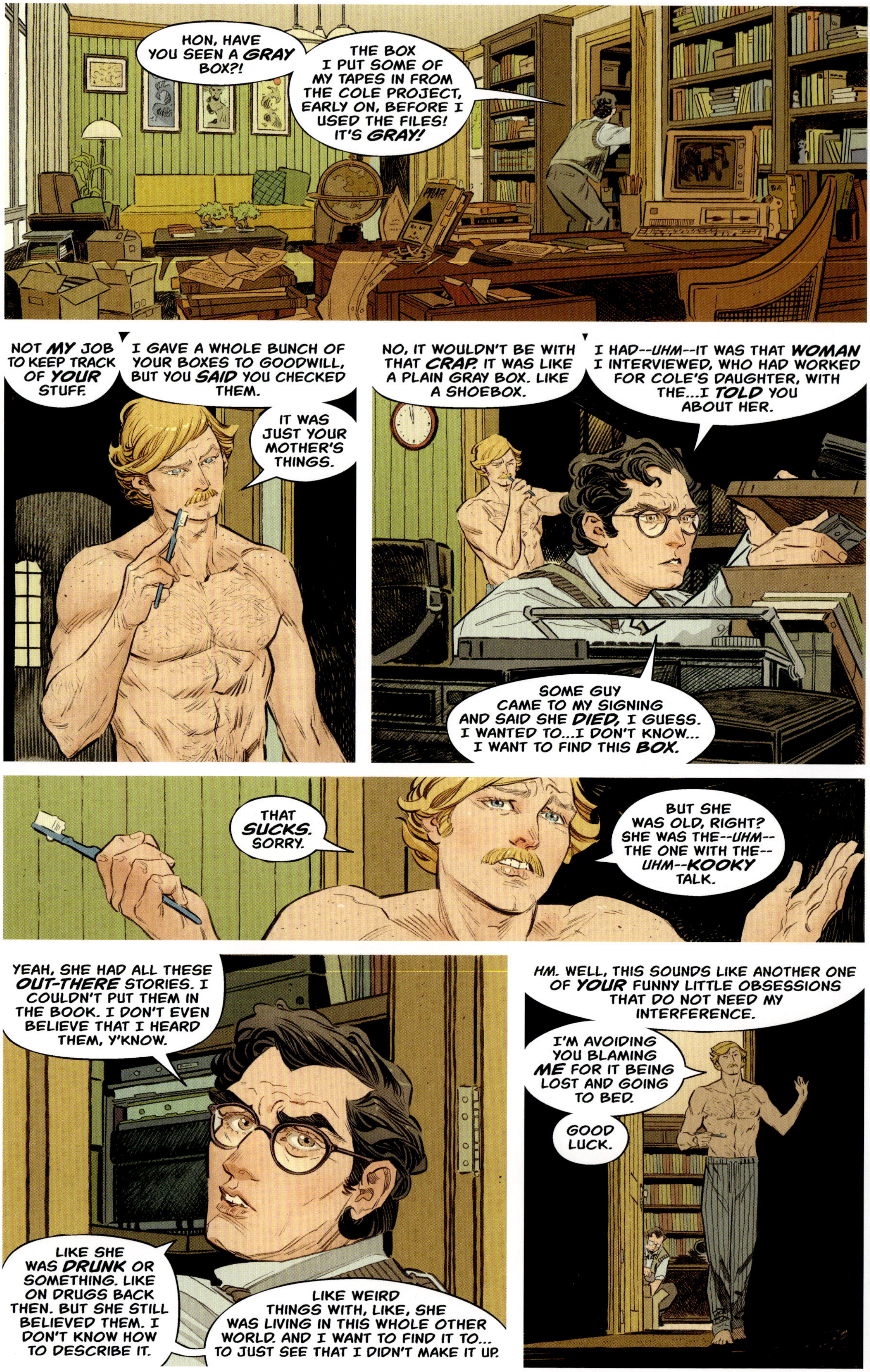
HON, HAVE YOU SEEN A GRAY BOX?!
THE BOX I PUT SOME OF MY TAPES IN FROM THE COLE PROJECT, EARLY ON, BEFORE I USED THE FILES! IT'S GRAY!
NOT MY JOB TO KEEP TRACK OF YOUR STUFF.
I GAVE A WHOLE BUNCH OF YOUR BOXES TO GOODWILL, BUT YOU SAID YOU CHECKED THEM.
IT WAS JUST YOUR MOTHER'S THINGS.
NO, IT WOULDN'T BE WITH THAT CRAP. IT WAS LIKE A PLAIN GRAY BOX. LIKE A SHOEBOX.
I HAD--UHM--IT WAS THAT WOMAN I INTERVIEWED, WHO HAD WORKED FOR COLE'S DAUGHTER, WITH THE...I TOLD YOU ABOUT HER.
SOME GUY CAME TO MY SIGNING AND SAID SHE DIED, I GUESS. I WANTED TO...I DON'T KNOW... I WANT TO FIND THIS BOX.
THAT SUCKS. SORRY.
BUT SHE WAS OLD, RIGHT? SHE WAS THE--UHM-- THE ONE WITH THE-- UHM--KOOKY TALK.
YEAH, SHE HAD ALL THESE OUT-THERE STORIES. I COULDN'T PUT THEM IN THE BOOK. I DON'T EVEN BELIEVE THAT I HEARD THEM, Y'KNOW.
LIKE SHE WAS DRUNK OR SOMETHING. LIKE ON DRUGS BACK THEN. BUT SHE STILL BELIEVED THEM. I DON'T KNOW HOW TO DESCRIBE IT.
LIKE WEIRD THINGS WITH, LIKE, SHE WAS LIVING IN THIS WHOLE OTHER WORLD. AND I WANT TO FIND IT TO... TO JUST SEE THAT I DIDN'T MAKE IT UP.
HM. WELL, THIS SOUNDS LIKE ANOTHER ONE OF YOUR FUNNY LITTLE OBSESSIONS THAT DO NOT NEED MY INTERFERENCE.
I'M AVOIDING YOU BLAMING ME FOR IT BEING LOST AND GOING TO BED.
GOOD LUCK.

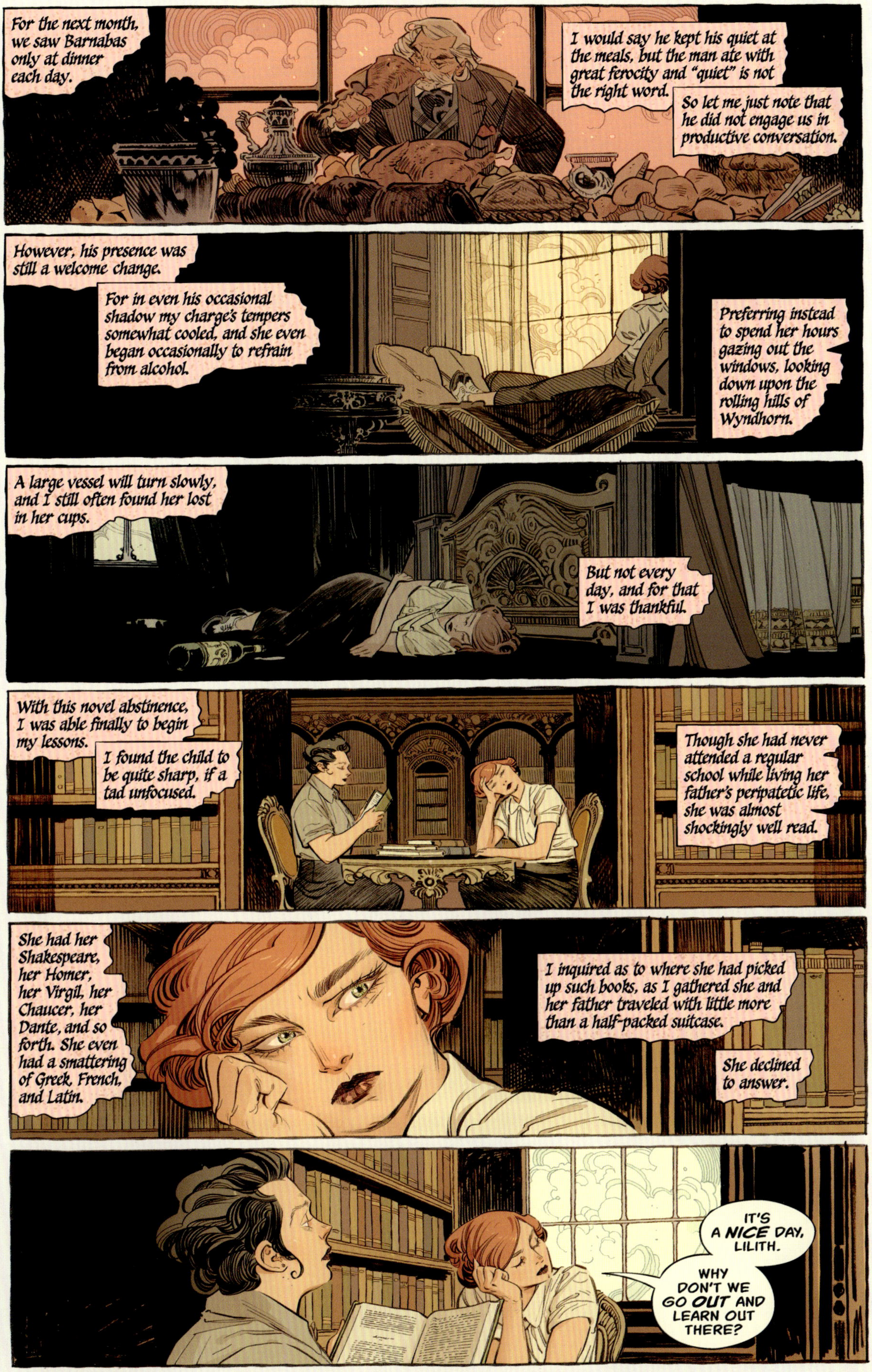

For the next month, we saw Barnabas only at dinner each day.
I would say he kept his quiet at the meals, but the man ate with great ferocity and "quiet" is not the right word.
So let me just note that he did not engage us in productive conversation.
However, his presence was still a welcome change.
For in even his occasional shadow my charge's tempers somewhat cooled, and she even began occasionally to refrain from alcohol.
Preferring instead to spend her hours gazing out the windows, looking down upon the rolling hills of Wyndhorn.
A large vessel will turn slowly, and I still often found her lost in her cups.
But not every day, and for that I was thankful.
With this novel abstinence, I was able finally to begin my lessons.
I found the child to be quite sharp, if a tad unfocused.
Though she had never attended a regular school while living her father's peripatetic life, she was almost shockingly well read.
She had her Shakespeare, her Homer, her Virgil, her Chaucer, her Dante, and so forth. She even had a smattering of Greek, French, and Latin.
I inquired as to where she had picked up such books, as I gathered she and her father traveled with little more than a half-packed suitcase.
She declined to answer.
IT'S A NICE DAY, LILITH.
WHY DON'T WE GO OUT AND LEARN OUT THERE?

Although I retained some trepidations as to what lurked in the shadows of Wyndhorn after the events of that horrible night...
...I did not dare raise these concerns to Helen and confirm in any way her paranoia.
And so I agreed to her suggestion.
Thus many of our lessons from that day on were conducted in the grounds and gardens of Wyndhorn.
Which were well kept and perfectly idyllic. And in the beginning, we encountered nothing more frightening than a flower.
But beginnings, like lives, are made to be lost. And so weeks later, we were... interrupted.
THERE'S SOMEONE ELSE HERE.
I did not have a clue as to what she was talking about. All I heard were the buzz of the insects and the vague poundings of Joseph beating at a carpet back at the house.
Before I could answer, she had sprinted off, leaving both me and her learning.
HELEN! WE ARE NOT FINISHED!
WE WILL HAVE A BREAK AT HALF PAST, AS WAS DISCUSSED EARLIER!
IT'S THIS WAY! AROUND THE BEND! ON THE OTHER SIDE OF THIS THING!
I am not some schoolmarm who prefers all forms of academics to any physicality.
I was on many a sports team in my youth, in fact, and prided myself on my foot speed.
But I could never catch that girl. There was a strength to her that seemed almost, well, savage.

Looking back, I do believe she got that from her grandfather.
OH.
YOU.
HELLO.

The master caught our attention then quickly looked back to his... his...I hesitate to label it.
His animal, one could say, if not accurately at least metaphorically.
HE'S HUNGRY.
I'M SORRY, SIR, WE SHOULD BE GETTING TO OUR STUDIES. WE DID NOT MEAN TO DISTURB YOU.
WHAT? IS THAT...
IT'S A FLYUNE?
YES. A YOUNG ONE.
YOUR FATHER TAUGHT YOU?
HELEN, THIS IS NOT THE TIME. YOU ARE EXPECTED ELSEWHERE.
LET US GO. NOW, DEAR.
NO...DAD NEVER...THEY'RE IN HIS STORY. THE STEEL MOUNTAIN. WHERE OTHAN...
I READ IT.
THIS WON'T HELP HER MUCH.
BUT SOME.
SHE NEEDS HER HEARTH.
WHERE'S THAT?

As I said, I never met your subject, the father, but between the grandfather and the granddaughter, my Helen.
There was a fair resemblance.
Something around the eyes.
YOUR STUDIES ARE IMPORTANT.
RETURN TO THEM.
GOVERNESS, SHE SHOULD BE INSIDE.
YES, OF COURSE, SIR. I ATTEMPTED TO TELL HER.
I'M SURE YOU HEARD ME. I HOPE.
BUT YES, SIR. OF COURSE, SIR.
GRANDFATHER!
WHAT ARE YOU?!

That night, Barnabas did not attend supper, and we ate alone.
Though I attempted to engage Helen in polite chitchat, she ignored my entreaties, and after the meal quickly retreated from the table.
Joseph and I made our usual search of the house and found her, defying our expectations, sober and in her room, where she begged for privacy.
I'M FINE! GOOD NIGHT!
Still, I expected her at my bedside by the midnight hour as was her daily custom, unbroken since our arrival.
And when she did not make her appearance by two hours past midnight, I became unusually worried.
I went back to her room to check on her well-being.
The door was locked, but I had long ago been provided with the key.
I expected, or I should say, I hoped to find her deep in slumber so that I might come and go without her knowing.
HELEN!
Sadly, this was not the case.
I DON'T HAVE ANY OF HIS BOOKS.

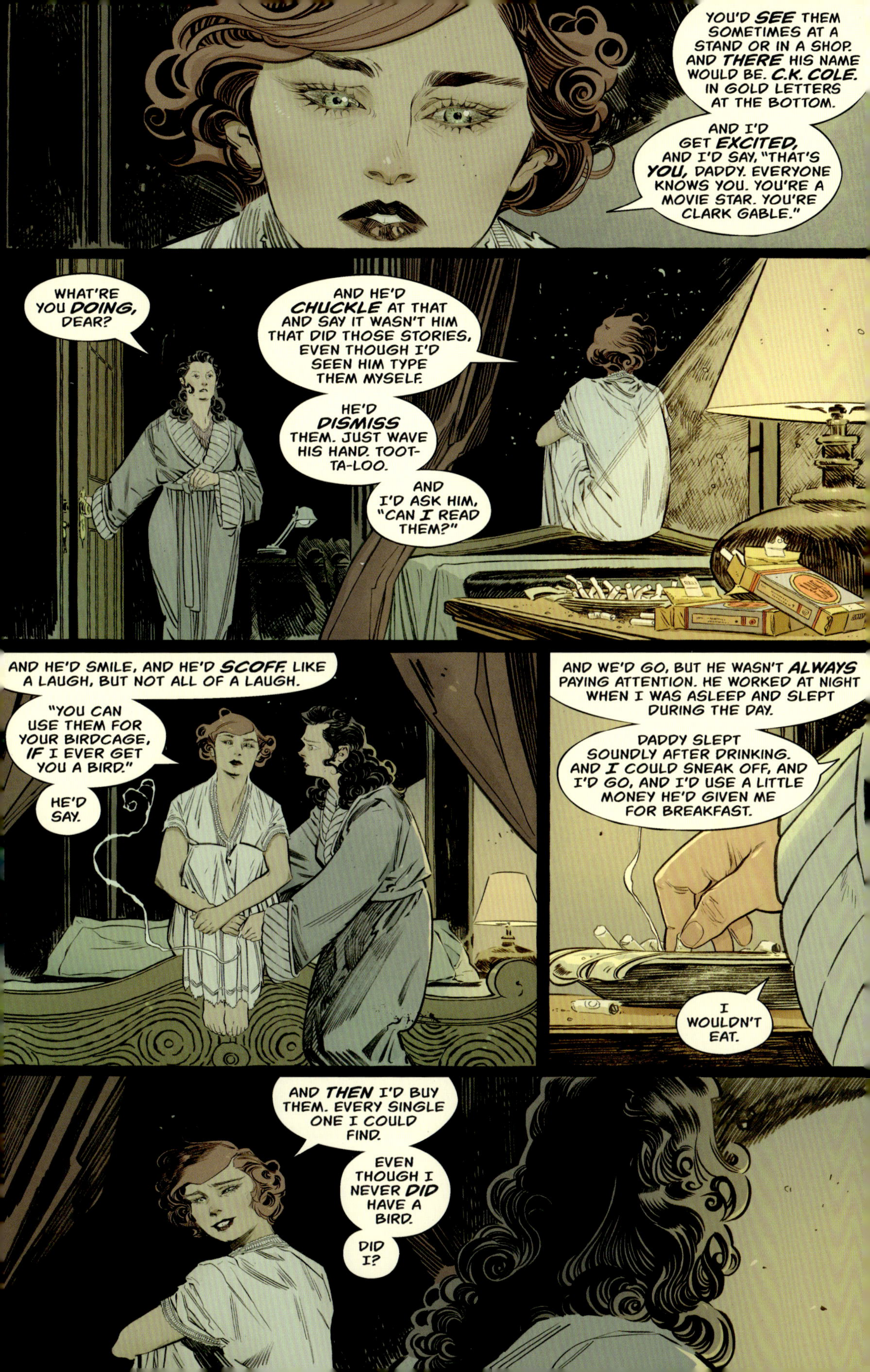
YOU'D SEE THEM SOMETIMES AT A STAND OR IN A SHOP. AND THERE HIS NAME WOULD BE. C.K. COLE. IN GOLD LETTERS AT THE BOTTOM.
AND I'D GET EXCITED, AND I'D SAY, "THAT'S YOU, DADDY. EVERYONE KNOWS YOU. YOU'RE A MOVIE STAR. YOU'RE CLARK GABLE."
WHAT'RE YOU DOING, DEAR?
AND HE'D CHUCKLE AT THAT AND SAY IT WASN'T HIM THAT DID THOSE STORIES, EVEN THOUGH I'D SEEN HIM TYPE THEM MYSELF.
HE'D DISMISS THEM. JUST WAVE HIS HAND. TOOT-TA-LOO.
AND I'D ASK HIM, "CAN I READ THEM?"
AND HE'D SMILE, AND HE'D SCOFF. LIKE A LAUGH, BUT NOT ALL OF A LAUGH.
"YOU CAN USE THEM FOR YOUR BIRDCAGE, IF I EVER GET YOU A BIRD."
HE'D SAY.
AND WE'D GO, BUT HE WASN'T ALWAYS PAYING ATTENTION. HE WORKED AT NIGHT WHEN I WAS ASLEEP AND SLEPT DURING THE DAY.
DADDY SLEPT SOUNDLY AFTER DRINKING. AND I COULD SNEAK OFF, AND I'D GO, AND I'D USE A LITTLE MONEY HE'D GIVEN ME FOR BREAKFAST.
I WOULDN'T EAT.
AND THEN I'D BUY THEM. EVERY SINGLE ONE I COULD FIND.
EVEN THOUGH I NEVER DID HAVE A BIRD.
DID I?

DO YOU KNOW THE HOUR, YOUNG LADY? WE CAN DISCUSS THIS ALL TOMORROW.
THE MONSTER, THE FLYUNE, TODAY-- LILITH, YOU WERE THERE, DID I SEE IT? I WAS A LITTLE DRUNK. I HAD A NIP THIS MORNING, YOU KNOW.
NOT SO MUCH.
I AM NOT ENTIRELY FAMILIAR WITH THIS COUNTRY. I SAW AN ANIMAL THAT WAS STRANGE TO ME. BUT IS THAT NOT TO BE EXPECTED?
I USED TO DREAM THEM.
AFTER I'D READ DADDY'S MAGAZINES, AND I'D COME BACK TO OUR ROOM, AND HE'D BE SNORING TO THE ROOF, AND I'D LAY DOWN.
AND I WASN'T SLEEPING LIKE HIM, BUT I WAS DREAMING THEM-- THE THINGS HE WROTE. THEY WERE INSIDE AND OUTSIDE.
NIGHT BRINGS ALL SORTS OF DEMONS OF WORRY.
LET US REVISIT THIS IN THE MORNING WHEN THE SUN CAN PROVIDE US WITH A TOUCH OF WARMTH FOR OUR SKIN AND SOUL.
DO YOU THINK DADDY WAS DREAMING THEM TOO WHILE I WAS NEXT TO HIM?
WERE WE HAVING THE SAME DREAMS?
WHEN HE DIED, WHERE DID HIS DREAMS GO?
HELEN, WOULD... WOULD YOU LIKE ME TO STAY? I CAN.
HERE.
UNTIL YOU'RE SETTLED.
YES.
I THINK THAT WOULD BE NICE.

I HAVE KEPT HER WORK *IN* THE MANOR THESE PAST WEEKS, AS YOU HAVE REQUESTED, AND THE GIRL HAS MADE *SOME* STRIDES.
BUT SHE IS...I HESITATE TO EVEN *RAISE* THE QUESTION WITH YOU, SIR, BUT I FEEL IT IS MY DUTY, AND I *CANNOT* FACE MY OWN NEGLECT.
SHE REQUIRES SOME...SOME MORE... SHE HAS *REQUIREMENTS* THAT ARE NOT BEING MET. TO HER *DETRIMENT*. IN MY OPINION.
SHE IS A GOOD GIRL. THAT IS NOT DOUBTED. NOT AN OUNCE.
BUT SHE...
SHE IS A *FINE* GIRL. BUT I BELIEVE YOU NOT BEING--
IS IT THE DRINK?
YES, WELL, I MEAN...
YES, *PARTIALLY*.
IT HAS DECREASED IN FREQUENCY, I WOULD SAY, BUT STILL OCCURS WITH SOME *MAGNITUDE*. BUT THE PROBLEM LIES DEEPER THAN--
THE GIRL IS *SIXTEEN*.
WHEN *I* WAS OF THAT AGE, I WAS IN THE DRINK FROM MORNING TO DUSK, DUSK TO MORNING.
I HAVE *SUCCEEDED*. SHE MAY DO SO AS WELL.
SHE MAY, YES, SIR. *SOME* DO. AS YOU HAVE.
BUT SOME DO *NOT*.
AS HER *FATHER* COULD, OR RATHER CAN *NO LONGER*, ATTEST.

CONTROL YOUR LIPS, WOMAN.
MY SON WAS NOT KNOWN TO YOU.
I...I AM AWARE OF SOME DETAILS. SIR.
I KNOW HE DRANK UNTIL HE WAS DEAD, AND SHE WATCHED HIM DO IT.
AND I KNOW A YOUNG GIRL LOOKS FOR PATHS TO FOLLOW, AND SHE HAS ONLY SEEN THIS ONE.
GET OUT.
SIR, WITH RESPECT, THE GIRL NEEDS TO--
WELL, I THINK SHE NEEDS TO SEE YOU. SHE NEEDS TO UNDERSTAND YOU--UNDERSTAND WHERE SHE IS AND WHO SHE IS.
WHAT IN GOD'S NAME ALL OF THIS IS.
I HAVE BEEN CHARGED WITH HER HEALTH AND EDUCATION. IT IS MY DUTY, AND IT IS SACROSANCT.
SHE MUST SEE ANOTHER PATH.
WHY MUST I ASK TWICE IN MY OWN HOUSE?!
GET OUT!

JESUS AND MARY!
WHY BRING HER HERE?!
DID YOU NOT HAVE THE PLEASURE TO WATCH YOUR SON FALL INTO HIS GRAVE?!
AND YOU HOPE SHE MIGHT HOST A REVIVAL OF THAT PARTICULAR ENTERTAINMENT?!
YOU...
GET OUT...
BARNABAS, I DIDN'T MEAN TO--
MY APOLOGIES. SHE'S A GOOD GIRL. IT'S ONLY...
JUST GO.
PLEASE.
I BEG YOU.

I could not sleep that night.
The words I'd said in anger to the master of the house kept somersaulting through my mind.
Who was that woman back there? Why did she rise when I always fall? Why did I--
I EXPECTED AT ANY MOMENT FOR JOSEPH TO RUSH TO ME TO TELL ME I HAD BEEN DISMISSED.
THAT HE DID NOT COME THAT EVENING DID NOT COMFORT ME IN THE SLIGHTEST.
AND I SPENT THE NEXT WEEKS IN A STATE OF REGRET AND ANXIETY. WHAT HAD I DONE?
WHAT SLY DEVIL POSSESSED ME TO TAKE SUCH A HARSH TONE WHEN--
CLICK
I FOUND HER NAME IN ONE RANDOM SAN ANTONIO POLICE RECORD OF WHO BAILED OUT COLE'S DAUGHTER AFTER HE DIED.
NO ONE HAD EVER ASKED HER ABOUT THIS. I DON'T THINK ANYONE EVER DID... LIKE AFTER.
SHE GOT MARRIED DURING THE WAR AND JUST...LIVED THAT LIFE.
I NEVER FOUND THIS JOSEPH OR... I MEAN, THE DAUGHTER AND THE GRANDFATHER AND WHAT HAPPENED TO THEM...
SHE WAS THE ONLY ONE THERE THAT COULD STILL TALK ABOUT IT. IT'S ALL GONE NOW. AND I DIDN'T PUT ANY OF IT IN. IT WAS, Y'KNOW, SHE'S CRAZY.
BUT, LIKE, HER STORY-- THERE'S NO ONE LEFT TO TELL IT.

In the weeks that followed, Helen grew worse. The drinking returned to its previous heights and she neglected her studies entirely.
The master of the house kept to himself and was seen only in glances as he passed from one room to another.
This all came to a pathetic climax the day we found her with the sword.
HEY, LILITH.
LOOK AT ME.
I'M A BARBARIAN.

This room was meant to be entirely off limits.
I still remember Joseph's voice that day. As if he'd kept this one picture of his true love for fifty years, and had just seen it pissed upon.
WHAT HAVE YOU DONE, GIRL?!
OH, HELEN, NO.
WOOOSH.
COME, MONSTERS! COME AND TEST THIS!
MY BLADE AWAITS YOUR FACE!
THE MASTER MUST BE INFORMED IMMEDIATELY!
GODS HELP US!
HELEN, DEAR, PUT DOWN THE SWORD, PLEASE.
ARE YOU A MONSTER, LILITH?!
DO YOU CHALLENGE ME?!
NO, DEAR.
I'M NOT ANY MONSTER.
I'M HERE TO TAKE CARE OF YOU. YOUR GRANDFATHER HIRED ME.
WHERE'S MY BIRD? DON'T I GET A BIRD?
...A BIRD IN A CAGE...
OH GOD.
IT'S ALL RIGHT, DEAR.
IT'S FINE.
I HAVE YOU.

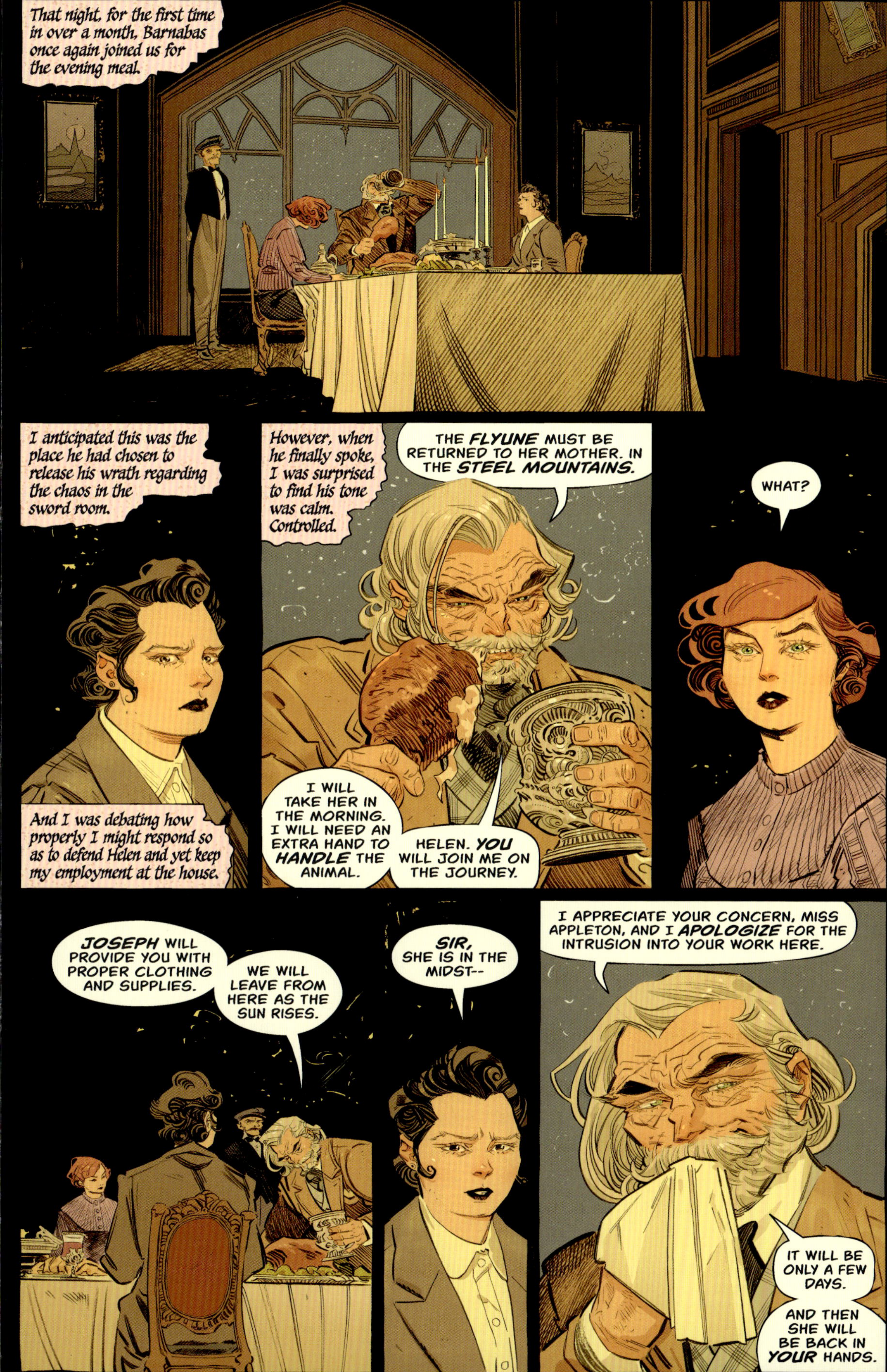
That night, for the first time in over a month, Barnabas once again joined us for the evening meal.
I anticipated this was the place he had chosen to release his wrath regarding the chaos in the sword room.
And I was debating how properly I might respond so as to defend Helen and yet keep my employment at the house.
However, when he finally spoke, I was surprised to find his tone was calm. Controlled.
THE FLYUNE MUST BE RETURNED TO HER MOTHER. IN THE STEEL MOUNTAINS.
I WILL TAKE HER IN THE MORNING. I WILL NEED AN EXTRA HAND TO HANDLE THE ANIMAL.
HELEN. YOU WILL JOIN ME ON THE JOURNEY.
WHAT?
JOSEPH WILL PROVIDE YOU WITH PROPER CLOTHING AND SUPPLIES.
WE WILL LEAVE FROM HERE AS THE SUN RISES.
SIR, SHE IS IN THE MIDST--
I APPRECIATE YOUR CONCERN, MISS APPLETON, AND I APOLOGIZE FOR THE INTRUSION INTO YOUR WORK HERE.
IT WILL BE ONLY A FEW DAYS.
AND THEN SHE WILL BE BACK IN YOUR HANDS.

The next morning, I watched from my window as grandfather and granddaughter stepped away from Wyndhorn and trekked into the forest.
In their absence, Joseph and I had conspired to search every nook and cranny of the house for the wine Helen had stolen.
We had no doubt it would be an arduous task, but we hoped for it to be fruitful.
I wonder now that I did not fear more for her on this, her first expedition to the lands beyond our own.
On subsequent trips, I would spend her leaving in a state of utter dread, fighting off all sorts of pernicious visions of her death.
I suppose the only answer to that quandary is that, at that time, I was blissfully ignorant of the dangers outside the manor.
And I assumed whatever awaited her out there might be better than the pain I prayed she'd leave behind.

Bilquis
Evely 23
Mat
Lopes

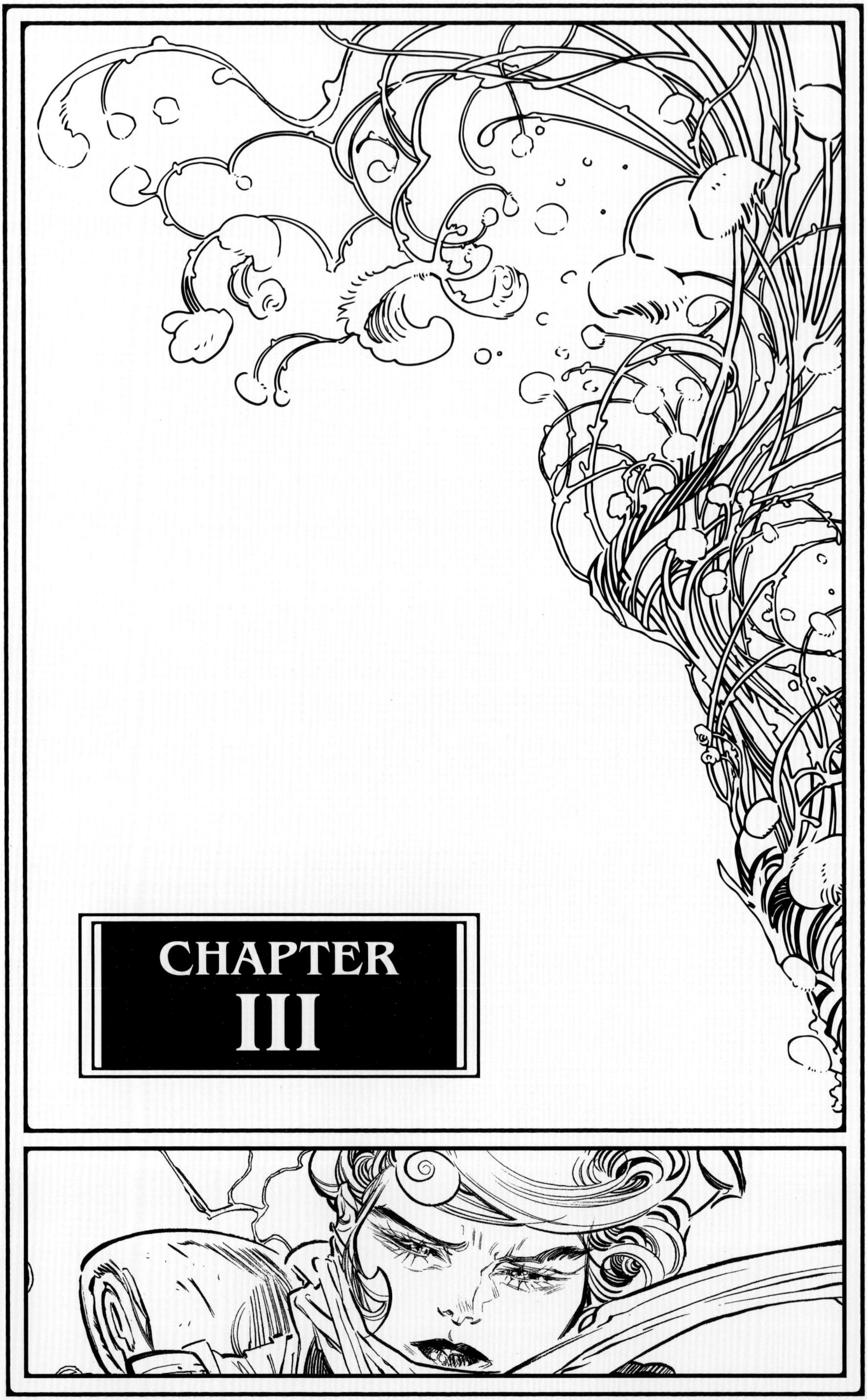
CHAPTER
III

THERE IS A REAL **WOW** FACTOR TO IT.
ESPECIALLY IN PERSON. LOOK AT THIS THING.
THE WORLD JUST COMES TO LIFE.
LIKE YOU CAN **TOUCH** IT.

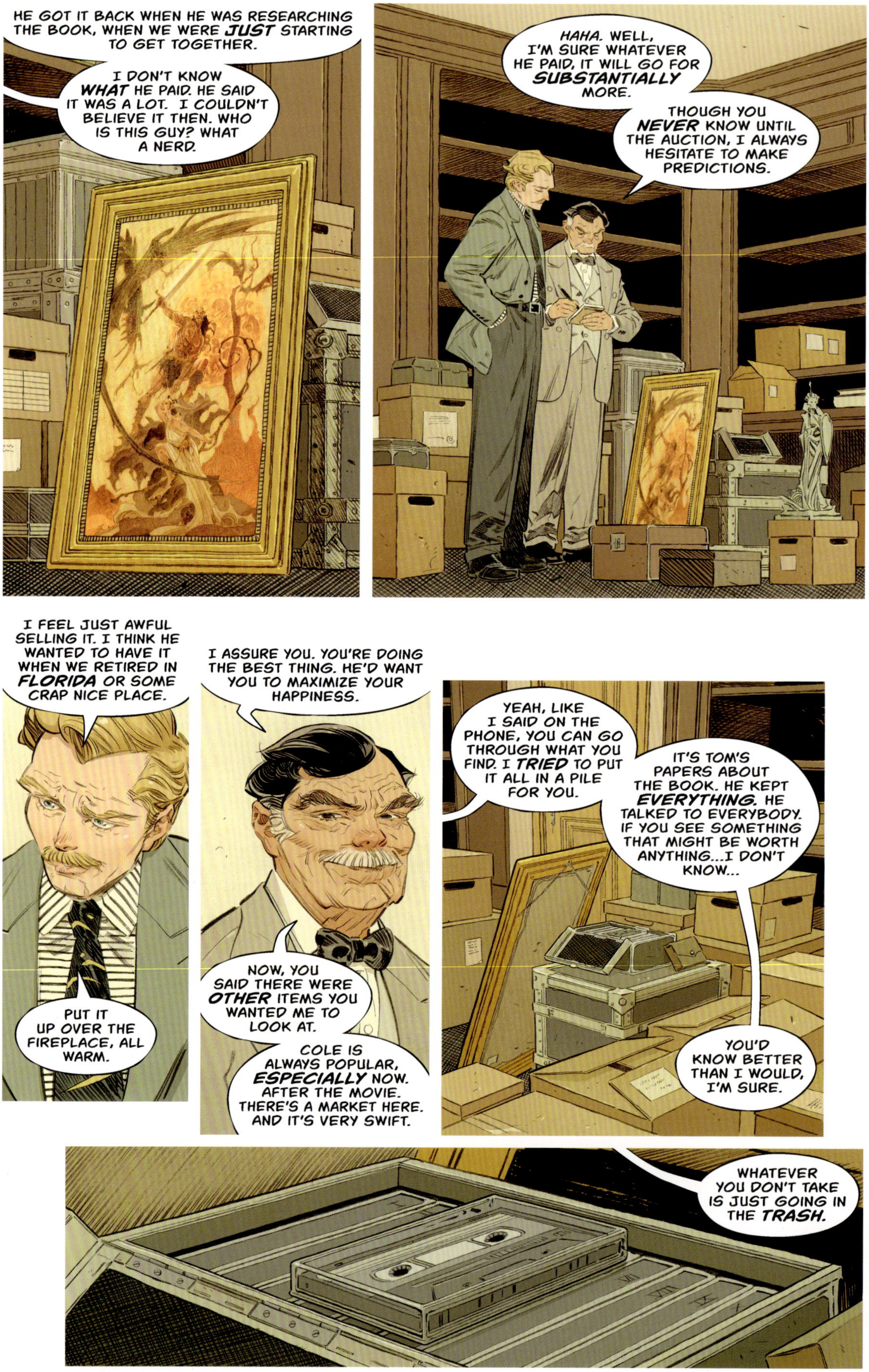
HE GOT IT BACK WHEN HE WAS RESEARCHING THE BOOK, WHEN WE WERE JUST STARTING TO GET TOGETHER.
I DON'T KNOW WHAT HE PAID. HE SAID IT WAS A LOT. I COULDN'T BELIEVE IT THEN. WHO IS THIS GUY? WHAT A NERD.
HAHA. WELL, I'M SURE WHATEVER HE PAID, IT WILL GO FOR SUBSTANTIALLY MORE.
THOUGH YOU NEVER KNOW UNTIL THE AUCTION, I ALWAYS HESITATE TO MAKE PREDICTIONS.
I FEEL JUST AWFUL SELLING IT. I THINK HE WANTED TO HAVE IT WHEN WE RETIRED IN FLORIDA OR SOME CRAP NICE PLACE.
PUT IT UP OVER THE FIREPLACE, ALL WARM.
I ASSURE YOU. YOU'RE DOING THE BEST THING. HE'D WANT YOU TO MAXIMIZE YOUR HAPPINESS.
NOW, YOU SAID THERE WERE OTHER ITEMS YOU WANTED ME TO LOOK AT.
COLE IS ALWAYS POPULAR, ESPECIALLY NOW. AFTER THE MOVIE. THERE'S A MARKET HERE. AND IT'S VERY SWIFT.
YEAH, LIKE I SAID ON THE PHONE, YOU CAN GO THROUGH WHAT YOU FIND. I TRIED TO PUT IT ALL IN A PILE FOR YOU.
IT'S TOM'S PAPERS ABOUT THE BOOK. HE KEPT EVERYTHING. HE TALKED TO EVERYBODY. IF YOU SEE SOMETHING THAT MIGHT BE WORTH ANYTHING...I DON'T KNOW...
YOU'D KNOW BETTER THAN I WOULD, I'M SURE.
WHATEVER YOU DON'T TAKE IS JUST GOING IN THE TRASH.

A month went by before I heard from Helen again.
LILITH!
NOTHING IS REAL!
I MEAN, NO, IT'S... EVERYTHING IS REAL!
I MEAN, I MEAN, YOU WON'T BELIEVE WHAT'S OUT THERE!
LILITH, I KILLED SOMEONE! THEN I DID IT AGAIN, BUT DON'T WORRY, IT WAS ALL NORMAL. OR EVEN BETTER THAN THAT!
HELEN.
THIS IS NOT THE PROPER PLACE TO GREET SOMEONE AFTER A JOURNEY, NOR THE PROPER TONE TO USE.
YOU HAVE RETURNED TO YOUR MANOR, YOU WILL ALSO RETURN TO YOUR MANNERS.
NOW, LISTEN--WHY DON'T YOU GET CHANGED FOR THE NIGHT? HAVE A GOOD SLEEP...
...AND WE WILL DISCUSS WHATEVER HAS HAPPENED BY THE LIGHT OF DAY?
YOU...
YOU'RE HERE!
I MADE IT!

I managed to get her into an outfit more suitable for the hour, but that, unfortunately, was as far as I got.
I found myself helpless to stop her rambling. Something inside her was pushing out and no dam I might build could hold it.
I DON'T KNOW WHERE TO START. IT'S CRAZY. IT'S LIKE IT ALL HAPPENED AT THE SAME TIME.
YES.
WELL, HOW ABOUT MR. COLE, IS YOUR GRANDFATHER WELL?
HAS HE, TOO, ARRIVED?
WE LEFT EACH OTHER AT THE EDGE OF THE FOREST. HE SAID FOR ME TO RUN AHEAD BECAUSE IT WAS SO LATE AND HE HAD TO CHECK ON THE STABLES.
BUT HE MADE IT BACK, HE'LL BE HERE SOON, I THINK. HE'LL BE FINE. HE'S FINE.
NOTHING CAN HURT HIM.
THAT SEEMS TO BE A TOUCH OF AN EXAGGERATION, DEAR. BUT I AM GLAD THE TWO OF YOU HAVE FOUND SOME CONNECTION.
I HAD HOPED FOR AS MUCH, BUT THERE SEEMED TO BE LEAGUES BETWEEN YOU WHEN YOU SET OUT.
I HAVE SEEN MONSTERS, LILITH.
AND GODS.
THERE ARE SO MANY GODS.
And with that casual and certainly despicable blasphemy, my charge began her tale of her journey abroad...
OH, HELEN, PLEASE.
...into lands fantastic and strange.

I followed Barnabas--Grandfather--toward the tree line to the east of the house, the view outside that window there. You know it.
I asked him over and over about where we were going, and he just did his grunting and kept telling me to hurry the Flyune up.
SHE DOESN'T WANT TO.
DOES SHE AT LEAST HAVE A NAME SO I CAN CALL HER?
NO.
"NO"? GREAT.
C'MON, NO! GOOD GIRL...FOLLOW ME.
LET'S GO. NO, NOW, YOU CAN DO IT! COME ON!
THAT'S A GOOD GIRL, NO.
OFF INTO THE FOREST WE GO AND OUT TO WHO THE HELL KNOWS WHERE?
DOESN'T THAT ALL SOUND LIKE IT'LL JUST BE A BARREL OF MONKEYS?

We walked on for what seemed to me to be hours. The trees were so thick, you couldn't even see the sun.
I don't really know how long it was.
I'M TIRED. MY LEGS HURT. CAN WE STOP?
NO.
YOU'RE FINE.
THAT'S STUPID.
YOU CAN'T TELL SOMEONE HOW THEY FEEL.
I KNOW MYSELF. I KNEW YOUR FATHER AND YOUR MOTHER.
THE BLOOD THAT IS IN YOU.
YOU'RE FINE.
DAD WAS A DRUNK WHO COULDN'T STOP. MOTHER WAS A WHORE WHO DIED HAVING ME.
I DON'T THINK THAT'S GOING TO HELP MUCH IN THE WOODS.
AND YET YOU KEEP WALKING.
AND JABBERING ON AND ON.
HOW TIRED COULD YOU BE?

I hate to admit it, but he wasn't completely wrong. I put one foot after the other and it was, I mean, it really was fine after a while.
I managed to keep pace with him for however many more miles it was. Until we finally found the small cabin.
Without saying anything, he led me inside. It was empty except for this madwoman sitting by herself on the floor.
OTHAN OF CASTLE HEIGHTS.
WHAT HAVE YOU BROUGHT ME?
IT IS BARNABAS OF WYNDHORN. AS YOU WELL KNOW, CRONE.
AND THIS IS MY GRANDDAUGHTER, HELEN.
MM. OF COURSE.
HOW PLEASANT. HOW MARVELOUS.
SHE LOOKS JUST LIKE THE GODDESS, DOESN'T SHE? UTTERLY REMARKABLE.
NO.
NNNN.
SHE LOOKS LIKE HER GRANDFATHER.

GOOD ENOUGH?
YOU BETTER HOPE SO, SWEETIE.
SOMEDAY I WILL COME HERE AND KILL YOU AND TAKE BACK WHAT YOU HAVE THIEVED FROM ME.
I WILL SMILE FOR A MONTH AFTER IN THE REMEMBERING OF IT.
REPEATING YOURSELF OVER AND OVER IS A SIGN OF SENILITY.
AS IS FORGETTING YOUR OWN NAME.
IGNORE HER. THOSE WHO WILL DIE BEFORE THEIR TIME WILL SPEND THEIR DAYS BEMOANING THEIR PATHETIC FATE.
JUST COME THROUGH HERE AND KEEP YOUR HAND UP, YOUR EYES SHADED.
WE HAVE WALKED IN THE SHADOW OF LEAVES, THEY WILL NOT BE ACCUSTOMED TO THE LIGHT.
JESUS, WHAT...

I went through the door and the trees were gone and the warmth hit my face.
COME.
WE WILL MAKE THE INN BY TWO DAYS' SUNDOWN.
Lilith, I didn't understand.
Any of it.
But Barnabas stepped forward into the sudden valley--into the new light.
And I followed.

We walked for many hours more. Longer than I have ever walked, even when Daddy and I were kicked off that train in Aberdeen.
YOUR GOVERNESS SAYS YOU DRINK.
By the time we got to the hotel, I was thirsty as all hell.
I GET BY.
It wasn't wine and it wasn't beer. It was sweet and earthy and pungent.
And powerful.
IS THERE MORE?
HEH.

SO YOU'RE *NOT* GOING TO TELL ME? ANYTHING? WHAT?
IS THAT *FAIR?* THAT'S NOT FAIR. *YOU* HAVE TO...IT'S NOT.
WHAT DO YOU WISH TO KNOW?
PFFT. THERE'S A WAY...A WAY THE WORLD *IS.* THERE ARE LAWS AND SCIENCES AND THESE THINGS... CAUSES. *EFFECTS.*
AND WE JUST...
WHERE IS THE...WHERE *ARE* WE?
WE SHOULD BE... WHAT...
ARE YOU FINISHED?
IS *THAT* YOUR LIMIT?
NO.
SILAS! TWO MORE HERE!
THE GIRL HAS A *PROUD* THIRST IN HER AND WE MAY YET *HONOR* IT!

I lay in the black for some time. Snug and warm.
Time passed for those who, unlike me, still cared about time.
MMM.
HELEN!
When I raised my head again, I was surrounded by the dead and the dying.
WHAT...
HURRY. SOME RAN. THEY WILL ALERT THE KING. MORE WILL COME.
WE DON'T HAVE TIME FOR THAT FILTH.
COME, LET'S OFF. TAKE THE ANIMAL. IT DOES NOT SEEM TO CARE FOR ME.

He doesn't like questions. I'm sure you've gathered that much.
It took the days of travel to learn what went on while my head rested on that very sticky table.
While I was floating in my cups, Barnabas continued drinking, which is almost unthinkable, honestly.
At some point a man came up to him, pointed at the young passed-out lady, me, and mocked my capacity for whatever that liquid was.
At which point, Barnabas stabbed the man in the throat.
I can't say if there was any warning or back-and-forth before that or exactly why he reacted as he did.
He was not at all clear about that part of the story.
Now, the man with the knife through his throat apparently had a brother who was sitting nearby and ran at Barnabas.
Barnabas grabbed the charging brother and threw him to the ground, then he stepped on the man's neck, snapping it.
After this, with two dead men at his feet, Barnabas apparently sat back down and had another pint.
Or four.
Which allowed enough time for the local guard troop, alerted by who knows who, to rush into the establishment and request he and I accompany them back to the stocks.
There were something near ten men in all who approached us.
Barnabas drew his sword.
And woke me a few minutes later.

I asked him if he was afraid more people would keep coming after him.
He said no. He said he'd been hunted before.
I said they could bring an army.
He said he had fought armies before.
I asked him then, "Are you afraid of anything?"
NO.

Weeks into our trek, I left the camp early in the morning to fetch water.
We drank mead every night, and I typically went down first. Barnabas would continue late into the evening, then sleep well past the sun rising.
That day he didn't even notice me leave.
I caught the stranger's reflection just as he was thrusting down his blade.
My dad and I slept in some low places over the years.
I wasn't unused to people trying to take advantage of situations.
My dad, though, was very strict about such incidents. If anything got that close and scared us that much, he'd say...
"Just run.
"Until we find someplace safe.
"Where we can hide."

But then, next to the water, after weeks of traveling with Barnabas.
AAAAHH!
I didn't run at all.
GUHHH
I just stayed there.
And I watched him die.
I don't know how long we lay all entwined together. Long enough that I was wet with his blood.
Eventually, I heard Barnabas laughing.
HAHAHAHAHA
STOP IT.
WILL YOU HELP ME?
NO. YOU ARE FINE.
JUST REMEMBER TO GRAB ONE OF HIS TEETH BEFORE YOU PUSH HIM INTO THE WATER.

A week or so later, we reached the Steel Mountains and began our climb.
The land was unforgiving, but as we went on, I found myself feeling oddly stronger with each step up.
There's something in the high air there, Lilith. It's fresher, crisper. It cools the heat in your lungs, but it doesn't cool you.
I didn't even want a cigarette, I just wanted to taste the air all the time.
It was actually Barnabas who called for the first rest.
PLEASE.
WE WAIT HERE. HAVE A DRINK.
DAD SAID YOU CLIMBED THIS MOUNTAIN FASTER THAN ANY MAN EVER HAD OR DREAMED. DURING THE CORSUCAN WAR.
YOU ARE GETTING OLD, OLD MAN.
HE DID, EH?
WELL, HE DIDN'T SAY IT. HE WROTE IT.
I THOUGHT IT WAS ALL JUST FOR FUN. OR MONEY, I GUESS.
BUT IT'S THIS.

I *DID* TAKE YOUR FATHER HERE.
ONCE. TO MEET HER.
HE DID NOT *CARE* FOR IT.
YEAH, HE WAS NEVER ONE FOR *EXERCISE*. NO.
I'M GUESSING THE TAVERN AND THE BEER WERE MORE OF WHAT *HE* WAS LOOKING FOR.
HELEN.
YOU *FOUND* HIM. AFTER HE...WENT HIS WAY.
I AM *TOLD* YOU FOUND HIM.
I... YEAH...YEAH, I DID.
HE ACTUALLY USED *MY* BELT. I FOUND *HIS* BROKEN ON THE FLOOR UNDER HIM. IT WAS POOR LEATHER. WE BOUGHT OUR STUFF FROM THIS SECOND-HAND SHOP.
LUCKY HE HAD GOTTEN ME A *NICER* ONE THAN HE GOT FOR HIMSELF. PAID A LITTLE EXTRA, I REMEMBER, TRYING TO BE *NICE*.
HM. YES.
HE WAS *NICE*.
AT TIMES.
I WILL DRINK *LATER*.
WE HAVE FAR TO GO.

We reached the summit after a few more days.
There were many uncanny sights in that time spent in those metal mountains.
Lions with tails of fire, a goat who spoke only three words but spoke them well, a boy with gold fingernails who said his name was Sunset.
But none compared to the woman we found all the way at the top.
YOU? HOW UNEXPECTED.
Liliith, she was...
LADY HEARTH.
ONE OF YOUR FLOCK WANDERED TO WYNDHORN.
I know my Bible. I'm not ignorant. But she...
DID SHE? THEY CAN BE SO UNRULY, ESPECIALLY AT THIS TIME OF YEAR.
WHO'S THE GIRL?
She was a god.
OUR GRANDDAUGHTER. HELEN.
WHAT?

I was so stunned, I let go the rope on the Flyune.
SHIT! WAIT!
SORRY!
IT IS ALL RIGHT, NO IS BACK WHERE SHE SHOULD BE.
THEY'RE LIKE US. THEY LONG TO BE FREE. AND THEY LONG TO BE HOME.
I DOUBT ALL THE STRENGTH OF OTHAN THE UNRIVALED COULD HOLD HER.
COME.
THIS IS NOT A PLACE FOR US TO LINGER.
BUT...
WAIT.
HE IS RIGHT. THERE IS DEATH HERE. FOR HIM. AND FOR YOU.
YOU MUST GO. AS QUICKLY AS YOU CAME.
I HOPE YOUR RETURNING IS PLEASANT, AND PLEASE GIVE MY LOVE TO JOSEPH.
GOODBYE, HELEN OF WYNDHORN.
THE BLESSED AND CURSED.

HE NEVER TOLD ME ABOUT YOU!
HE NEVER TOLD ME ANYTHING!
I don't know if she heard me or if she just didn't care.
I shouted. She left.
And soon, I was alone.
I found Barnabas not half a mile down the mountain puffing air in and out. As worn and rough as I'd ever seen him.
With the steady shake creeping into his voice and body, I could have easily mistaken his exhaustion for fear.
IT IS D-DONE.
GOOD.
You should've been there, Lilith. It's hard to describe. It isn't the man we know.
I WILL TAKE THAT WATER NOW.
For a second, he was more...
He was a bit like my father, I think.

The way back was as eventful as the way there.
That army did finally catch up to us and I got to see Barnabas keep his word and beat them into the ground.
There were monsters and maggots and swamps and swords.
And in between it all we'd stop and we'd drink and we'd laugh.
I didn't ask him about the woman or about Father or about how none of it made any sense at all.
I kept my questions and he kept his answers.
And it was all so wonderful.

And that was Helen's story. As it was told that day by my bed, her eyes blazing when they should have been closed and away.
She had left distraught, seen a god, and returned in a fit of almost girlish giggles.
YOU ABUSE ME.
This trip seemed to change--
"MS. APPLETON."
NOT AS MUCH AS YOU DESERVE.
"YES?"
HOW DO YOU--
THEY ARE PULLED ALWAYS FROM ENEMIES, I PALM ONE AND GIVE IT TO HER. SHE PROBABLY KNOWS, BUT SAYS NOTHING.
IT'S A GAME WE PLAY.
"I WANT TO BE HONEST WITH YOU. I'M ENJOYING THIS, I AM.
"I JUST...I DON'T UNDERSTAND. THIS IS A SERIOUS BOOK I'M WORKING ON. MAYBE YOU DON'T UNDERSTAND. I'M NOT LOOKING FOR FICTION OR YOUR...WHATEVER THIS IS."
AND, UH.
IS SHE MY MOTHER?
"I'M TRYING TO FIND OUT ABOUT C.K. COLE. WHAT HAPPENED TO HIM. TO HIS DAUGHTER. HOW THEY DIED. AND THIS, THIS WHOLE...FANTASY.
"ARE YOU TRYING TO WASTE MY TIME?"
HAHA HAHAHA HAHA

ALL RIGHT, OUR NEXT ITEM UP, NUMBER 3773 IN YOUR CATALOG, IS A GROUP OF TAPES. A VERY UNIQUE GROUP OF TAPES, I THINK.
WELL WORTH YOUR TIME.
THESE ARE FROM THE ESTATE OF **THOMAS ROGERS,** THE OFFICIAL BIOGRAPHER OF **C.K. COLE,** THE AUTHOR OF THE *OTHAN* TALES, OFTEN CALLED THE "FATHER OF FANTASY."
THESE ARE A **SERIES** OF TAPED INTERVIEWS ROGERS MADE WITH THE FAMILY AND FRIENDS OF **COLE.**
NOW **COLE** IS A VERY MYSTERIOUS FIGURE, AS YOU WELL KNOW. HE KILLED HIMSELF **JUST** BEFORE GETTING POPULAR. HANGED HIMSELF.
AND THESE ARE **KEY** TAPES IN UNLOCKING WHO HE WAS.
THIS COULD BE A REAL **TREASURE** FOR THE RIGHT COLLECTOR.
THE HOUSE HAS LISTENED TO THE TAPES. THEY ARE IN **GOOD** SHAPE. VERY CLEAR. VERY INTERESTING IS MY UNDERSTANDING.
COMPLETELY **UNIQUE.** MOST OF THESE PEOPLE HAVE PASSED ON. A WINDOW INTO A LOST WORLD, YOU MIGHT THINK OF IT.
VERY, **VERY** INTERESTING STUFF.
WE'LL START AT FIVE HUNDRED.
WHICH IS A **STEAL.**
WHO WILL GIVE ME **FIVE HUNDRED?**
I'M TELLING YOU, FOLKS, THIS IS A ONE-OF-A-KIND **OPPORTUNITY.** NO ONE KNOWS WHAT YOU'RE GOING TO FIND.

Bilquis Evely '23
Mat Lopes

CHAPTER
IV

KEY ISSUE, GOOD PRICE, DISPLAYS REAL WELL.
FIRST APPEARANCE OF SARRA.
YOU AN OTHAN FAN? HE'S OUT OF FAVOR BECAUSE OF P.C. CRAP NOW, WITH ALL THESE STUPID PEOPLE SCREAMING ABOUT WHO'S OFFENDED.
BUT IF YOU LIKE THIS ONE, I'VE GOT SOMETHING REAL SPECIAL OVER HERE.
YOU WON'T EVEN BELIEVE IT.

THESE I PICKED UP AT AUCTION. WASN'T EVEN SURE WHAT THEY WERE.
$10
START BALOOM GROUP
SO OTHAN WAS CREATED BY C.K. COLE, RIGHT?
DUDE WHO HUNG HIMSELF, YOU KNOW? IN THE PULP DAYS. YOU KNOW ABOUT THAT?
YEAH. LIKE IN THE '40s OR SOMETHING.
NO, THIS IS THE '30s. BEFORE WORLD WAR II, EVEN.
THAT GUY HAD THE MOON, YOU KNOW, AND THEN WHAT'D HE HAVE?
BUT MAYBE THAT'S WHY HE HAD IT. MAYBE THE ONLY WAY YOU GET IT IS 'CAUSE YOU LOSE IT, I DON'T KNOW.
ANYWAY, THERE WAS A BOOK ABOUT IT. BY THIS DUDE.
AND I BOUGHT THE DUDE'S MATERIALS HE WAS USING. ESTATE STUFF.
IT'S NOT MY THING, I HAVEN'T GONE THROUGH IT ALL, BUT IT COULD BE...WHO KNOWS.
HOW MUCH WOULD YOU PAY FOR THAT?
WHAT DO YOU THINK? CAN WE MAKE A DEAL HERE?

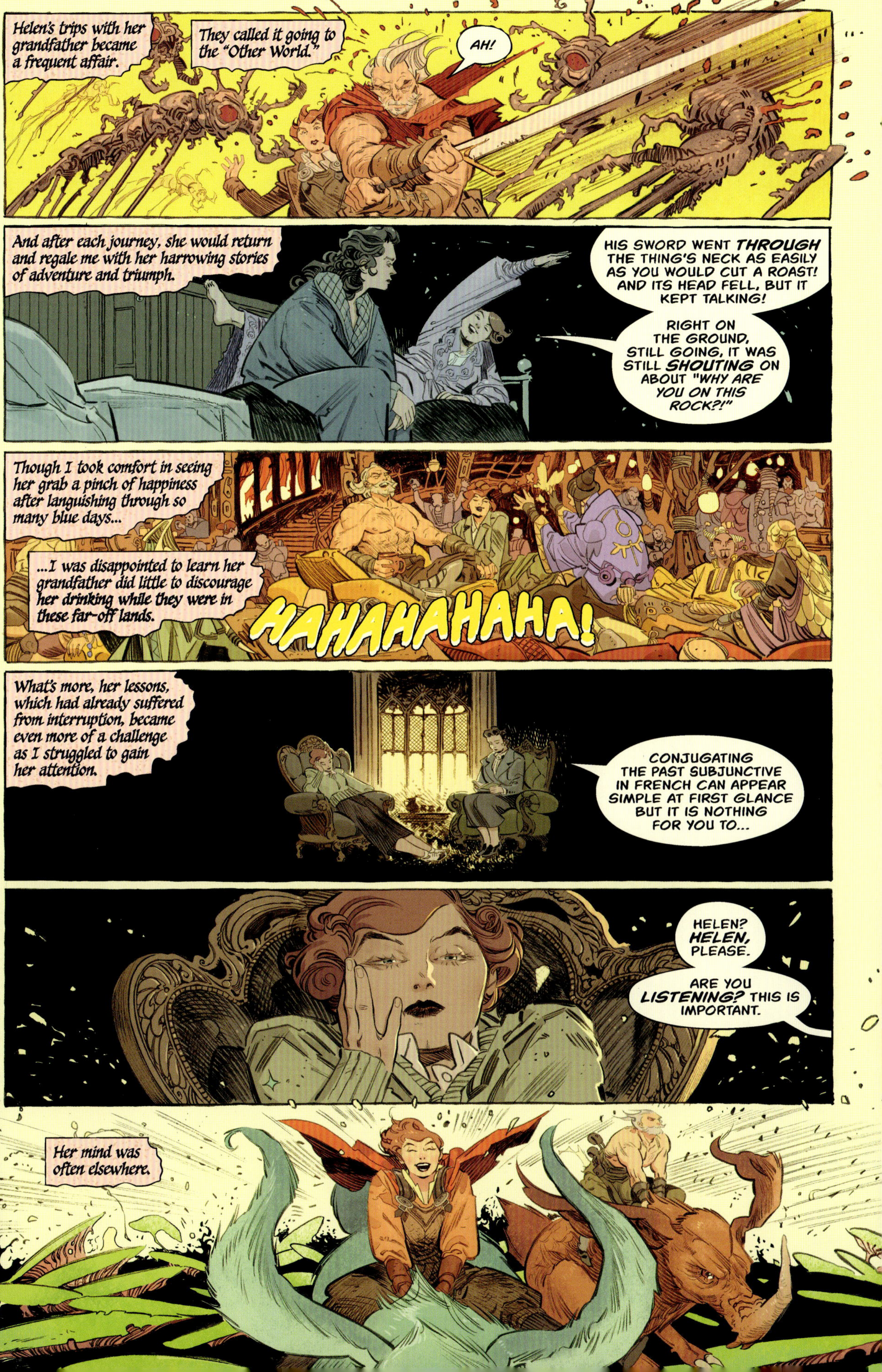

Helen's trips with her grandfather became a frequent affair.
They called it going to the "Other World."
AH!
And after each journey, she would return and regale me with her harrowing stories of adventure and triumph.
HIS SWORD WENT **THROUGH** THE THING'S NECK AS EASILY AS YOU WOULD CUT A ROAST! AND ITS HEAD FELL, BUT IT KEPT TALKING!
RIGHT ON THE GROUND, STILL GOING, IT WAS STILL **SHOUTING** ON ABOUT "WHY ARE YOU ON THIS ROCK?!"
Though I took comfort in seeing her grab a pinch of happiness after languishing through so many blue days...
...I was disappointed to learn her grandfather did little to discourage her drinking while they were in these far-off lands.
HAHAHAHAHAHA!
What's more, her lessons, which had already suffered from interruption, became even more of a challenge as I struggled to gain her attention.
CONJUGATING THE PAST SUBJUNCTIVE IN FRENCH CAN APPEAR SIMPLE AT FIRST GLANCE BUT IT IS NOTHING FOR YOU TO...
HELEN? **HELEN,** PLEASE.
ARE YOU **LISTENING?** THIS IS IMPORTANT.
Her mind was often elsewhere.

I WANT TO LEARN TO FIGHT LIKE YOU DO.
I'VE READ TOO MANY OF DADDY'S STORIES OF THESE WOMEN IN DANGER AND ALL OF THEM HIDING BEHIND YOU AS THE GROSS, ROTTEN THINGS COME.
THOSE WEREN'T THE FUN STORIES. I DIDN'T REALLY LIKE THOSE TYPES OF WOMEN. I DON'T THINK DADDY EVEN UNDERSTOOD THEM.
I WANT TO BE LIKE SARRA THE PIRATE QUEEN. WITH HER SUN-DIPPED SCIMITAR FORGED AT THE BOTTOM OF THE ORC'S TRENCH.
I NEED TO...SWING INTO BATTLE AND STAB MY OPPONENTS, NOT JUST TURN AWAY AND SCREAM FOR YOU AND HOPE FOR THE BEST.
I WANT TO BE GOOD. REALLY.
HELEN, YOUR GRANDFATHER LIVES A LIFE VERY DIFFERENT FROM YOUR OWN.
YOU CANNOT EXPECT HIM TO--
JOSEPH, YOU WILL TRAIN THE GIRL.
START AFTER THE MEAL. YOU HAVE ONE YEAR FROM THIS DAY.
REALLY?!
MR. COLE!
YES, SIR. I WILL SEE IT DONE.

Sure enough, as he forever did and would, Joseph followed his master's instruction to a tee.
CAN YOU REACH THE BRANCH?
NO, I DON'T THINK SO.
JOSEPH, THIS IS ABSURD. AT LEAST LET THE GIRL SLEEP IN HER OWN BED TONIGHT.
I WILL LIFT YOU ONCE. AFTER, IF YOU FALL, YOU WILL FIND YOUR OWN WAY UP. CLIMB, JUMP, FIND A STOOL, I DON'T CARE.
ALL RIGHT.
HELEN, LET'S GO TO SLEEP, DON'T BOTHER YOURSELF WITH THIS FOLLY.
GRIP THE BRANCH, A GOOD GRIP.
I HAVE IT.
WE CAN DISCUSS ALL OF THIS LATER. WE ARE RUSHING WHEN THERE IS NO NEED.
IT HURTS.
IT'S SUPPOSED TO. THE PAIN MEANS YOUR GRIP IS CORRECT.
HANG AS LONG AS YOU CAN. WHEN YOU FALL, GET BACK UP AND HANG AGAIN. I WILL CHECK ON YOU IN THE MORNING.
WHAT?!
SEE YOU BRIGHT AND EARLY. BRING COFFEE.
JOSEPH! YOU COME BACK HERE RIGHT NOW!
JOSEPH!
DON'T YOU DARE IGNORE ME! I WILL REPORT THIS BEHAVIOR TO THE MASTER OF THE HOUSE!

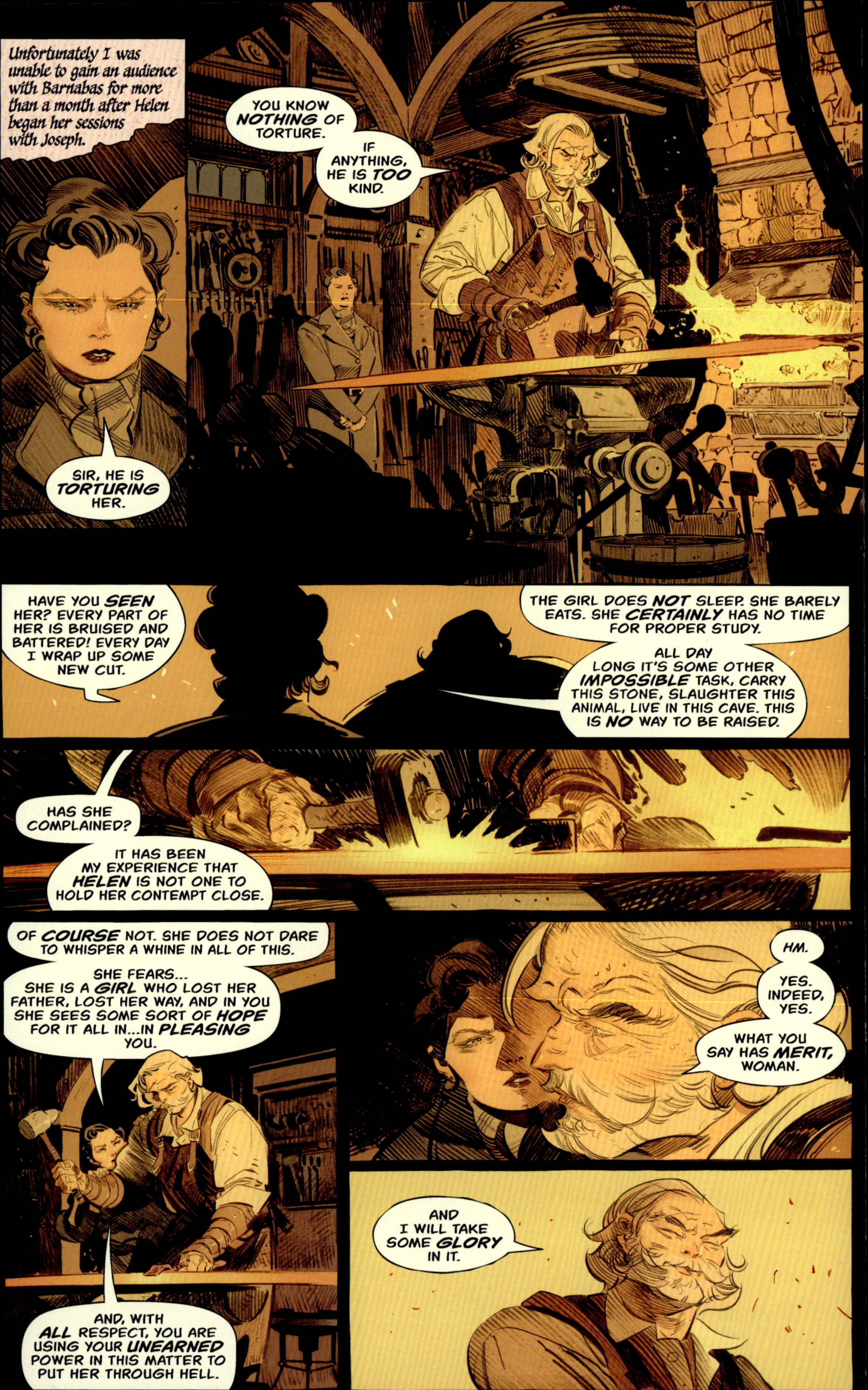
Unfortunately I was unable to gain an audience with Barnabas for more than a month after Helen began her sessions with Joseph.
SIR, HE IS TORTURING HER.
YOU KNOW NOTHING OF TORTURE.
IF ANYTHING, HE IS TOO KIND.
HAVE YOU SEEN HER? EVERY PART OF HER IS BRUISED AND BATTERED! EVERY DAY I WRAP UP SOME NEW CUT.
THE GIRL DOES NOT SLEEP. SHE BARELY EATS. SHE CERTAINLY HAS NO TIME FOR PROPER STUDY.
ALL DAY LONG IT'S SOME OTHER IMPOSSIBLE TASK, CARRY THIS STONE, SLAUGHTER THIS ANIMAL, LIVE IN THIS CAVE. THIS IS NO WAY TO BE RAISED.
HAS SHE COMPLAINED?
IT HAS BEEN MY EXPERIENCE THAT HELEN IS NOT ONE TO HOLD HER CONTEMPT CLOSE.
OF COURSE NOT. SHE DOES NOT DARE TO WHISPER A WHINE IN ALL OF THIS.
SHE FEARS... SHE IS A GIRL WHO LOST HER FATHER, LOST HER WAY, AND IN YOU SHE SEES SOME SORT OF HOPE FOR IT ALL IN...IN PLEASING YOU.
AND, WITH ALL RESPECT, YOU ARE USING YOUR UNEARNED POWER IN THIS MATTER TO PUT HER THROUGH HELL.
HM.
YES. INDEED, YES.
WHAT YOU SAY HAS MERIT, WOMAN.
AND I WILL TAKE SOME GLORY IN IT.

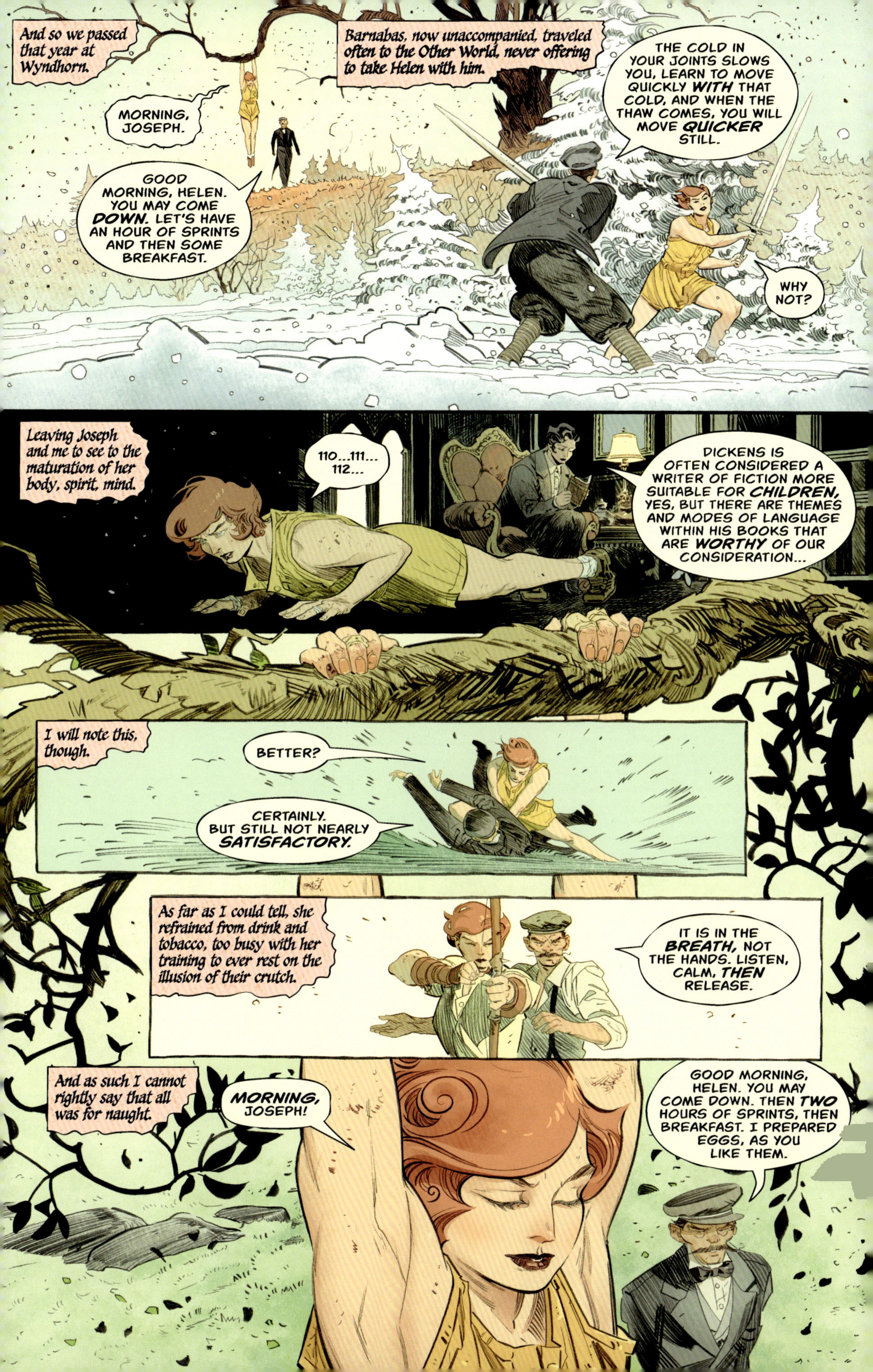

And so we passed that year at Wyndhorn.
MORNING, JOSEPH.
GOOD MORNING, HELEN. YOU MAY COME DOWN. LET'S HAVE AN HOUR OF SPRINTS AND THEN SOME BREAKFAST.
Barnabas, now unaccompanied, traveled often to the Other World, never offering to take Helen with him.
THE COLD IN YOUR JOINTS SLOWS YOU. LEARN TO MOVE QUICKLY WITH THAT COLD, AND WHEN THE THAW COMES, YOU WILL MOVE QUICKER STILL.
WHY NOT?
Leaving Joseph and me to see to the maturation of her body, spirit, mind.
110...111... 112...
DICKENS IS OFTEN CONSIDERED A WRITER OF FICTION MORE SUITABLE FOR CHILDREN, YES, BUT THERE ARE THEMES AND MODES OF LANGUAGE WITHIN HIS BOOKS THAT ARE WORTHY OF OUR CONSIDERATION...
I will note this, though.
BETTER?
CERTAINLY. BUT STILL NOT NEARLY SATISFACTORY.
As far as I could tell, she refrained from drink and tobacco, too busy with her training to ever rest on the illusion of their crutch.
IT IS IN THE BREATH, NOT THE HANDS. LISTEN, CALM, THEN RELEASE.
And as such I cannot rightly say that all was for naught.
MORNING, JOSEPH!
GOOD MORNING, HELEN. YOU MAY COME DOWN. THEN TWO HOURS OF SPRINTS, THEN BREAKFAST. I PREPARED EGGS, AS YOU LIKE THEM.

From the moment I had first met her, Helen had shown confidence in only one aspect of her life.
I LIKE THE SWORD.
IT'S WHAT EVERYONE IN THE OTHER WORLD USES.
Her own destruction.
I HAVE BEEN TRAINING YOU THESE MANY SEASONS. YOUR SKILL LIES IN THE AXE. THAT IS WHAT YOU WILL CARRY AND WHAT YOU WILL USE.
WHAT YOU LIKE OR DISLIKE IS OF NO CONSEQUENCE WHATSOEVER.
NOW READY YOURSELF.
However, day by day, month by month, she was beginning to discover a justified pride in her exceptional, though sometimes rude, willfulness.
FINE.
AXES. WHOOPEE.
READY AND WAITING. SIR.
Perhaps she was not learning her French as well as she might have, but she was learning, nonetheless.
NOW REMEMBER, THERE IS ONE KEY TO THIS EXERCISE.
DO NOT ALLOW ME TO KILL YOU.

And so, a year to the day from her first request, Helen stood in the entrance hall of Wyndhorn house adorned in weapons and armor.
She looked quite at home, I thought.
SO, GRANDPA.
DO YOU LIKE IT?
Not her home, perhaps. But close enough.

JOSEPH.
SHE DID WELL. SHE'S A HARD WORKER.
I THINK YOU WILL BE PLEASED.
YES.
HOWEVER.
GIVEN YOUR PREVIOUS FAILURE, JOSEPH...
...FORGIVE ME FOR NOT RELYING ON YOUR THOUGHTS.
THAT'S NOT VERY NICE.
YOU COULD'VE TAKEN MY HEAD.
BUT I GUESS YOU'LL FORGIVE ME THEN, OLD MAN, IF I, TOO, DISPENSE WITH NICETIES.
AND TAKE YOURS INSTEAD.
HEH.

As the two of them played their toddlers' game, I sidled up to Joseph seeking pertinent tidbits.
It had been my experience that Barnabas rarely, if ever, spoke of the past, and I was curious what his oblique reference to a failure meant.
Joseph, forever being Joseph, attempted to deflect me with invitations to observe the fracas.
But as I had no interest in it, I was persistent in my pursuit and eventually wore him far enough down to get the wisp of an answer.
"The son," he hissed at me.
"There was an attempt made to remediate that sickly boy. But what could be done, eh?"
He said no more, and seemed suddenly impervious to my further inquiries.

ENOUGH!
DID I...
QUIET!
JOSEPH CAN TEACH YOU MANY THINGS.
LET ME TEACH YOU THIS ONE.
A WARRIOR HAS NO NEED FOR WORDS.
OH.
OKAY. I MEAN--
SORRY. YEAH. OKAY. GOOD. SORRY.

Helen and Barnabas left that night.
They did not say when they would return.
I gave some thought to leaving myself, to finding a pupil and parents that would appreciate my efforts.
After all, what is a governess to do with no one to govern?
But I quickly dismissed this petite rebellion. I had been handed a mission and been paid handsomely, and I intended to see it to its end, whatever that might be.
I recalled spying the girl for the first time in that jail cell and thinking how many before me must have failed her to bring her so low.
I had no intention of being another in that long line of frauds.
With nothing better to do, I began dusting one of the rooms, though to be honest they were all well kept.
Joseph, for all his many flaws, was exacting in his cleanliness.
And then, with very little warning, a surprising but powerful sob ran through me, and I found tears pouring from my eyes.
I had as much explanation for it as I had control over it.
And in the absence of Helen, I stood in the middle of that large room.
And wept.

She returned from the Other World five weeks later.
Though she attempted to wear a cloak of stoic calm in the presence of her grandfather, I could tell she was happier than I'd ever seen her.
And sure enough, she rushed into my room that very night, the story of her adventure bursting out of her.
She told me they journeyed to the Forgotten Caves of the Well Witches...
...where it was rumored the priceless Silver Tongue of Glackus had fallen.
There, they found a woman named Callubaraux who entertained them for days.
Until she discovered their true intent and transformed into a giant insect in an attempt to stop the two thieves.
The battle raged for hours and was lost and won a dozen times, but in the end it was Helen herself who delivered the final, fatal blow.
I DID IT!
BUT DID YOU GET THE...WHATEVER? THE SILVER THING? YOUR **TONGUE?**
I DON'T **KNOW,** WHO CARES?!

And so another few seasons passed.
With Helen and Barnabas sometimes at the house.
And sometimes not.
"I'm his equal now," she told me once as she sat in the tub and I tried to scrub the dried blood from her back and neck.
"The Other World is mine and his, and we share it. I've never loved anything more."
Her late father was no longer mentioned.

I am sad to say that this respite of growth and occasional contentment did not last as long as any of us might have willed it.
KNOCK KNOCK KNOCK
I AM COMING! PLEASE! I'M HERE!
One night, I was awakened by a frantic knocking. I dashed to the door, performing Joseph's duties for neither the first nor the last time.
KNOCK KNOCK KNOCK
ONE MOMENT, LET ME--
What I saw when I finally managed to get that stubborn door open sickened me.
To this very day, this very moment, the memory brings a hint of bile to my throat. I taste it now as I speak to you.
JESUS, MARY, AND JOSEPH.
HUSH WITH THAT, WOMAN. THERE IS A LIFE AT STAKE IN OUR QUICK ACTION.
AND WE HAVE NO TIME FOR YOUR IMPOTENT GODS.
FETCH JOSEPH, IMMEDIATELY.

I did as I was told and rounded up Joseph while Barnabas carried the fallen and bruised Helen to her room.
SHE NEEDS A CAPABLE DOCTOR.
Hours of anguish then passed as we did nothing but wait.
HER WOUNDS WERE SUSTAINED IN COMBAT WITH STRANGE FORCES.
JOSEPH KNOWS MORE ABOUT THESE INJURIES THAN ANYONE ALIVE OR DEAD. IT'S THE BEST WE CAN DO, AND SO WE SHALL DO IT.
My anger at that moment got the best of me, I am unashamed to say.
JOSEPH?! JOSEPH IS THE DAMN BUTLER!
Barnabas had clearly endured his own pain in this battle, but refused to retire from Helen's side to treat his own lacerations.
JOSEPH IS MANY THINGS.
Instead, he kept by the door and, unlike me, kept his calm.
IS THAT HOW YOU WILL EXPLAIN IT IF THE GIRL DIES?!
WE DIDN'T CALL A DOCTOR BECAUSE THE MAN WHO MAKES THE BEDS HAS OTHER SKILLS?! I'M SURE THAT MAKES IT ALL DANDY!
Which I found rather frustrating, to be honest.
HELEN CANNOT DIE.
I WILL NOT ALLOW IT.

Despite my many protestations, I was not permitted into the room for three days. Only Joseph stayed by her side.
WHAT *IS* IT? IT SMELLS AWFUL.
Finally, he determined that she had passed some incomprehensible threshold, and I was granted access to my charge.
IT'S FROM *JOSEPH,* HE SAYS YOU'RE TO HAVE A CUPFUL EVERY HOUR ON THE HOUR, REMEMBER?
IT WILL MAKE YOU *BETTER,* HE SAYS. AND YOU HAVE COME THIS FAR, SO...SO *DRINK* UP. NO CHOICE IN THE MATTER.
GOOD, EXCELLENT, WELL DONE.
NOW YOU JUST *REST,* MY DEAR, AND I WILL WAKE YOU WHEN MORE MEDICINE IS REQUIRED.
LILITH...
THERE WERE *MEN,* LILITH, MEN WITH WINGS, LIKE ANGELS, SO MANY... CLOUDS OF THEM, HUNDREDS OF ANGELS AROUND...
BUT LILITH, THEY...THEY WEREN'T ANGELS... WERE THEY?
SHHHH. NO TIME FOR *THAT* TALK. JUST CLOSE YOUR EYES AND REST. YOU NEED YOUR *STRENGTH* MORE THAN I NEED YOUR VOICE.
LIE BACK, SIT *STILL.*
I'LL BE HERE.
DADDY KNEW...HE JUST...LILITH, HE WOULDN'T...
...HE DIDN'T WRITE...ABOUT THE ANGELS...

When she was able, Helen relayed to me her woeful tale.
They had climbed the Mountain of Thorns and found themselves at the entrance to a castle made entirely of diamonds.
As they stepped off the rock and toward the castle, they heard a massive flapping, as if a dozen flocks of birds were suddenly descending upon them.
They looked up.
It was not birds.
The ambush was swift and unrelenting. Dozens of winged warriors swarmed around them, slashing their steel, determined to kill the intruders.
And these were not wild trolls madly stabbing at a danger, these were trained soldiers executing a specific and terminal maneuver.
Helen believed the battle lost before it began. The creatures were simply too numerous,
Nonetheless, they fought.
It was violence as she had never experienced before. Everywhere she swung them, her axes hit flesh, and she pulled the blades back through bone.
After some time, she could not say how long, she was able finally to look around and see that they stood alone, granddaughter and grandfather among a sea of dead men.
Then she collapsed and remembered nothing more.

Recovery took months.
In all that time, the master of the house was either away traveling or locked in one of his various rooms.
He never saw Helen.
It was only when she could walk and we were enjoying a stroll on the grounds during one of our lessons that she finally spied her grandfather.
And not a second later, her joy knowing no bounds, she ran to him as fast as her newly repaired legs might carry her.
BARNABAS! BARNABAS!
BARNABAS!
I'M BETTER! I'M READY! I WORKED AND I PUT MYSELF TOGETHER! ALL THE PIECES, IT'S ALL... I'M GOOD AGAIN!
AND JOSEPH HELPED AND SO DID LILITH, AND I'M READY, WE CAN GO OUT AND FIND THEM!
ALL THOSE BASTARDS WHO DID THIS TO US! I'VE BEEN DREAMING OF IT!
THERE IS NO NEED TO RETURN TO THEM.
THEY AND THEIR KINGDOM ARE NO MORE.

I BROUGHT YOU THE HEAD OF THE HAWK KING.
YOU MAY DISPOSE OF IT OR MOUNT IT, IT IS YOUR DECISION.
BUT...
I THOUGHT WE'D DO IT TOGETHER, WE FOUGHT TOGETHER. WE ALMOST...
MAYBE THERE'S MORE...WE COULD... TRY THE BALARIAN HILLS...NEAR DEATH'S HALLOW IN CYTHIA...
NO.
YOU ARE DONE WITH TRAVELING.
TAKE THIS AND GO HOME. WE WILL SPEAK AT SUPPER.
I DON'T UNDERSTAND. I'M FINE. LIKE YOU ALWAYS SAY. FINE.
BUT DONE? NO. WHAT DOES THAT EVEN MEAN?
YOU FAILED.
YOU WILL STAY HERE. YOU WILL LEARN FROM YOUR GOVERNESS.
WHEN YOU ARE FINISHED, YOU WILL FIND A HUSBAND AND YOU WILL LEAVE.
WHAT?
TAKE HER AWAY, WOMAN.
I HAVE DUTIES IN WYNDHORN AND HAVE NO TIME NOW FOR HYSTERICS.

DAMN YOU!
THIS IS THE HEAD OF A ONCE POWERFUL GOD.
IT IS NOT AN OBJECT TO BE TRIFLED WITH IN SUCH A MANNER.
I'M NOT ANOTHER @$%@$% SWORD!
YOU CAN'T USE ME AND TOSS ME IN A @$%@ ROOM FOR YOUR COLLECTION!
YOU WILL NOT USE SUCH TONE AND LANGUAGE HERE.
WHAT HAS BEEN DONE WAS DONE FOR YOU.
OH, IS THAT WHAT YOU SAID TO MY FATHER WHEN YOU ABANDONED HIM?
WAS THAT HIS LAST THOUGHT AS HIS NECK SNAPPED IN THAT RAT-INFESTED MOTEL?
"WHAT HE DID, HE DID FOR ME."
I THOUGHT YOUR FATHER HAD STRENGTH, JUST AS I THOUGHT YOU DID.
ON BOTH OCCASIONS, I WAS PROVEN WRONG. THAT IS NO REASON FOR THIS OUTBURST.
YOU...
YOU BASTARD...

YOU DON'T KNOW A @$%$&#@ THING ABOUT MY FATHER!

MY MOM'S ON THE WAY, SHE'S GOING TO PULL INTO THE FRONT THERE, CALL WHEN SHE'S HERE.
WHAT'S THE BEST THING YOU GOT?
TOM'S
I SPENT, LIKE, A TON AT THE ONE-DOLLAR BINS.
I GOT, LIKE, THREE RUNS I'D BEEN LOOKING FOR. ONLY MISSED, LIKE, FIVE ISSUES.
NICE.
OTHAN
BUT NOT OTHAN #37! FIRST APPEARANCE OF SARRA. KEY ISSUE.
I GOT IT AS A DEAL WITH THIS OTHER STUFF. JUST ONE FIFTY.
COOL.
WHAT'S THE OTHER STUFF?
IT WAS, LIKE, THESE TAPES, MAN, THEY'RE CRAZY, I GOT THEM HERE.
THE DUDE SAID IT WAS, LIKE, THE TRUE STORY OF--LIKE NO ONE ELSE KNOWS IT, BUT THIS IS THE TRUTH OF WHAT HAPPENED TO C.K. COLE.
WHY HE KILLED HIMSELF.
WHAT?
WHO THE @$%$ IS C.K. COLE?

Bilquis Evely '23
Mat Lopes

CHAPTER
V

YOUR STEPFATHER WANTS THIS MAN CAVE. WHAT DO YOU WANT ME TO DO?
MA, THERE MUST BE SOME PLACE FOR IT.
IT'S YOUR JUNK, WHY AM I SUPPOSED TO FIGURE IT OUT?
WHAT ABOUT THE GARAGE? IS IT WET?
WHAT DO YOU MEAN, IS IT WET? AM I A THERMOMETER NOW?

WHAT? A THERMOMETER? I'M SAYING IT CAN GET MOLD, MA. I DON'T WANT TO COME HOME AND THEY'VE ALL GOT THAT SMELL.
OTHAN
START BALOOM GROUP
YOUR STEPFATHER SAYS IF WE DONATE THEM, WE GET A GOOD BREAK ON THE TAXES.
HE'S BEEN LOOKING AT THEM ON GOOGLE.
MOM, JUST LEAVE IT ALONE. IF HE WANTS A MAN CAVE, JUST HAVE THEM IN THERE OR PUT THEM WHERE THERE'S SPACE.
LITTLE NERDS
COSMIC
IT'S, LIKE, MY WHOLE CHILDHOOD. AND THERE'S STUFF IN THERE THAT'S WORTH, LIKE, ACTUAL REAL MONEY.
NOT, LIKE, A LOT, BUT I DON'T KNOW. JUST KEEP IT.
RON WANTS THIS FOOTBALL THING. HE'S NOT GOING TO GET THIS. HE DOESN'T EVEN LIKE THE MOVIES, AND I LIKE THEM.
HE SAYS WE CAN GET A DEAL. SHOULDN'T WE DO THAT?
MA, JUST PLEASE DON'T, OKAY? PLEASE?
I REALLY LOVE THAT STUFF, SERIOUSLY. IT'S IMPORTANT TO ME, OKAY? I DON'T EVEN KNOW WHAT ALL OF IT IS.

After that, Helen started drinking again.
OPEN THE GODDAMN DOOR!
THE MASTER'S ORDERS ARE THAT THE ARMORY IS TO BE LOCKED WHILE HE IS AWAY.
THIS IS NOT A TOPIC FOR DISCUSSION.
HELEN, LET'S GO LIE DOWN. YOU COULD OPEN YOUR STITCHES IF YOU GET TOO EXCITED.
DO YOU KNOW, JOSEPH, I KILLED THREE OF THE FOUR OWL PRINCES OF JOKCLAHYME? THE FOURTH ONE KILLED HIMSELF WHEN HE SAW ME COMING.
MAYBE YOU SHOULD OPEN THAT DAMN DOOR.
YOU ARE DRUNK. YOUR GOVERNESS IS RIGHT.
GO WITH HER BEFORE YOU CAUSE YOURSELF TROUBLE.
DO YOU KNOW WHAT I'VE DONE? IN THE OTHER WORLD? WITH TWO AXES YOU GAVE ME?
IS THREATENING ME SO SMART, JOSEPH? I DON'T KNOW...
IT IS NOT MY HOUSE. I DO NOT SET THE RULES, BUT I ABIDE BY THEM.
I ADVISE YOU TO DO THE SAME.

Later, without my prompting, Joseph explained to me that he knew very well how Helen had fared with the Owl Princes.
Indeed, he found it to be greatly impressive.
AAAH!
The Owl Dynasty was embedded entirely in a hierarchy of violence...
...and each member of the royal family spent their life preparing for the moment when they would have to kill the others.
THERE IS NO BENEFIT TO THIS.
GNNN
That she downed one of these paranoid men was enough for a poem in their lands. Three was unprecedented.
Which explained the suicide of the fourth.
At this admission, Joseph smiled at me, and I could not help but see the immense egotism in his visage.
It was, after all, he who had nursed this fire inside Helen.
Then the smile dropped and he noted that the reason there were so many Owl Princes was that the King, who controlled them all, had been assassinated a few years prior.
A true feat of strength, given the King's long streak of victory in hand-to-hand battle.
FINE. JOSEPH.
It had been a tricky murder, he claimed.
But nonetheless he had pulled it off.
THERE'S MORE FUN SOMEWHERE ELSE.

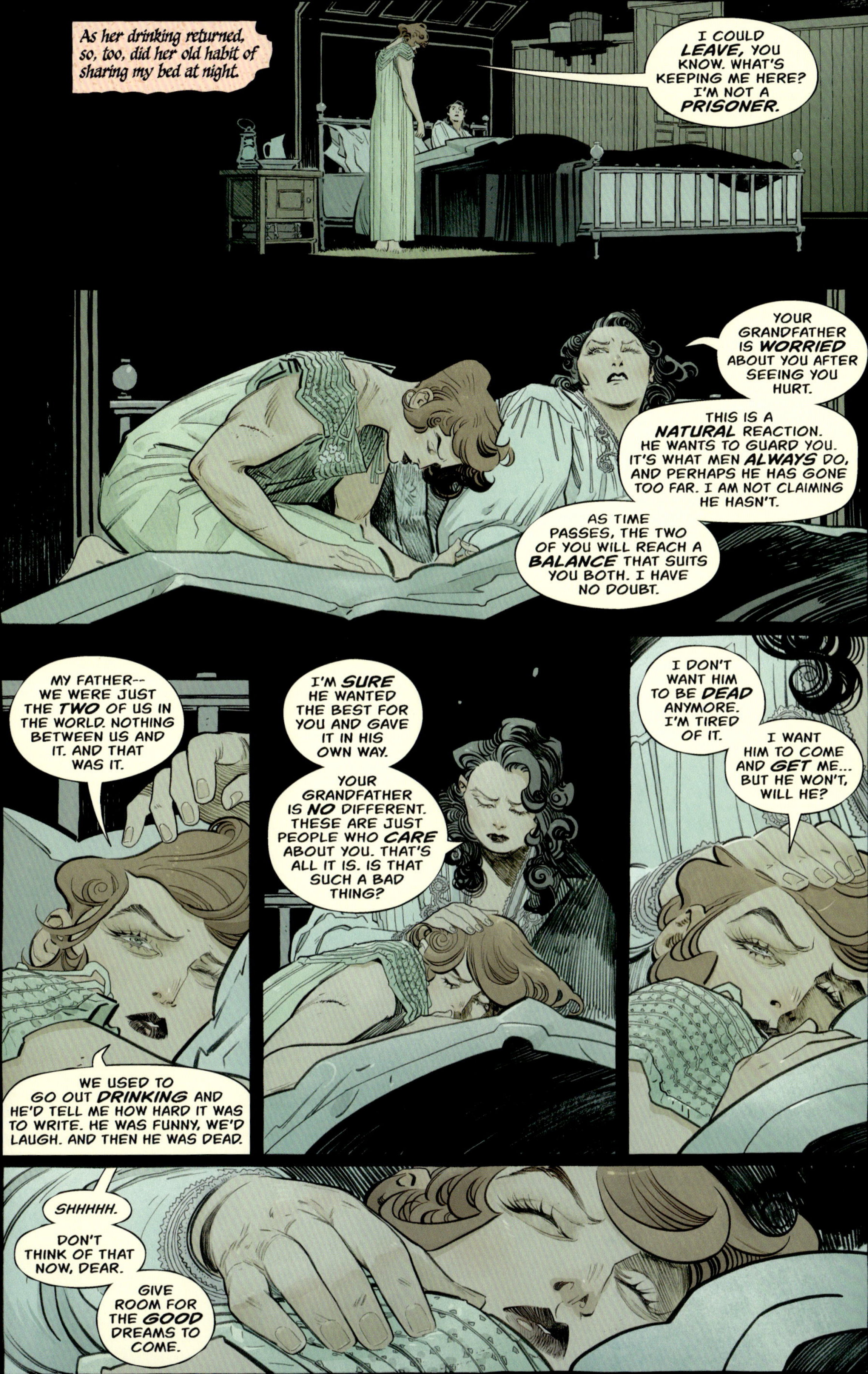

As her drinking returned, so, too, did her old habit of sharing my bed at night.
I COULD LEAVE, YOU KNOW. WHAT'S KEEPING ME HERE? I'M NOT A PRISONER.
YOUR GRANDFATHER IS WORRIED ABOUT YOU AFTER SEEING YOU HURT.
THIS IS A NATURAL REACTION. HE WANTS TO GUARD YOU. IT'S WHAT MEN ALWAYS DO, AND PERHAPS HE HAS GONE TOO FAR. I AM NOT CLAIMING HE HASN'T.
AS TIME PASSES, THE TWO OF YOU WILL REACH A BALANCE THAT SUITS YOU BOTH. I HAVE NO DOUBT.
MY FATHER-- WE WERE JUST THE TWO OF US IN THE WORLD. NOTHING BETWEEN US AND IT. AND THAT WAS IT.
WE USED TO GO OUT DRINKING AND HE'D TELL ME HOW HARD IT WAS TO WRITE. HE WAS FUNNY. WE'D LAUGH. AND THEN HE WAS DEAD.
I'M SURE HE WANTED THE BEST FOR YOU AND GAVE IT IN HIS OWN WAY.
YOUR GRANDFATHER IS NO DIFFERENT. THESE ARE JUST PEOPLE WHO CARE ABOUT YOU. THAT'S ALL IT IS. IS THAT SUCH A BAD THING?
I DON'T WANT HIM TO BE DEAD ANYMORE. I'M TIRED OF IT.
I WANT HIM TO COME AND GET ME... BUT HE WON'T, WILL HE?
SHHHHH.
DON'T THINK OF THAT NOW, DEAR.
GIVE ROOM FOR THE GOOD DREAMS TO COME.

When I woke the next day, Helen was gone and there was blood on the pillow and sheets.
It did not take a great leap of the imagination to guess where she had now gone.
I quickly threw on some clothes and sprinted outside into the cool morning air.
HELEN!
To my relief she had not yet made it to the forest, though she showed no signs of slowing despite certainly hearing my pleas.
HELEN! YOU WILL WAIT THERE! HELEN!
As I previously noted, I am not a woman who quails from physical activity, and I have confidence in my own strength.
But to catch Helen that day I had to push my legs beyond anything they had ever before attempted, and I could feel the objection of my body in my lungs and throat.
HH HH HH
Nonetheless, I got to her before she entered the tree line.
HH HH HH
ARE YOU ALL RIGHT?
I had no instinct to argue with her to come back.
I had lost enough such bickers in the past. I knew the only way for me to help was to forge ahead.
I AM FINE.
JUST OLDER THAN I THOUGHT I WAS. AND WHAT A TRAGEDY THAT IS.

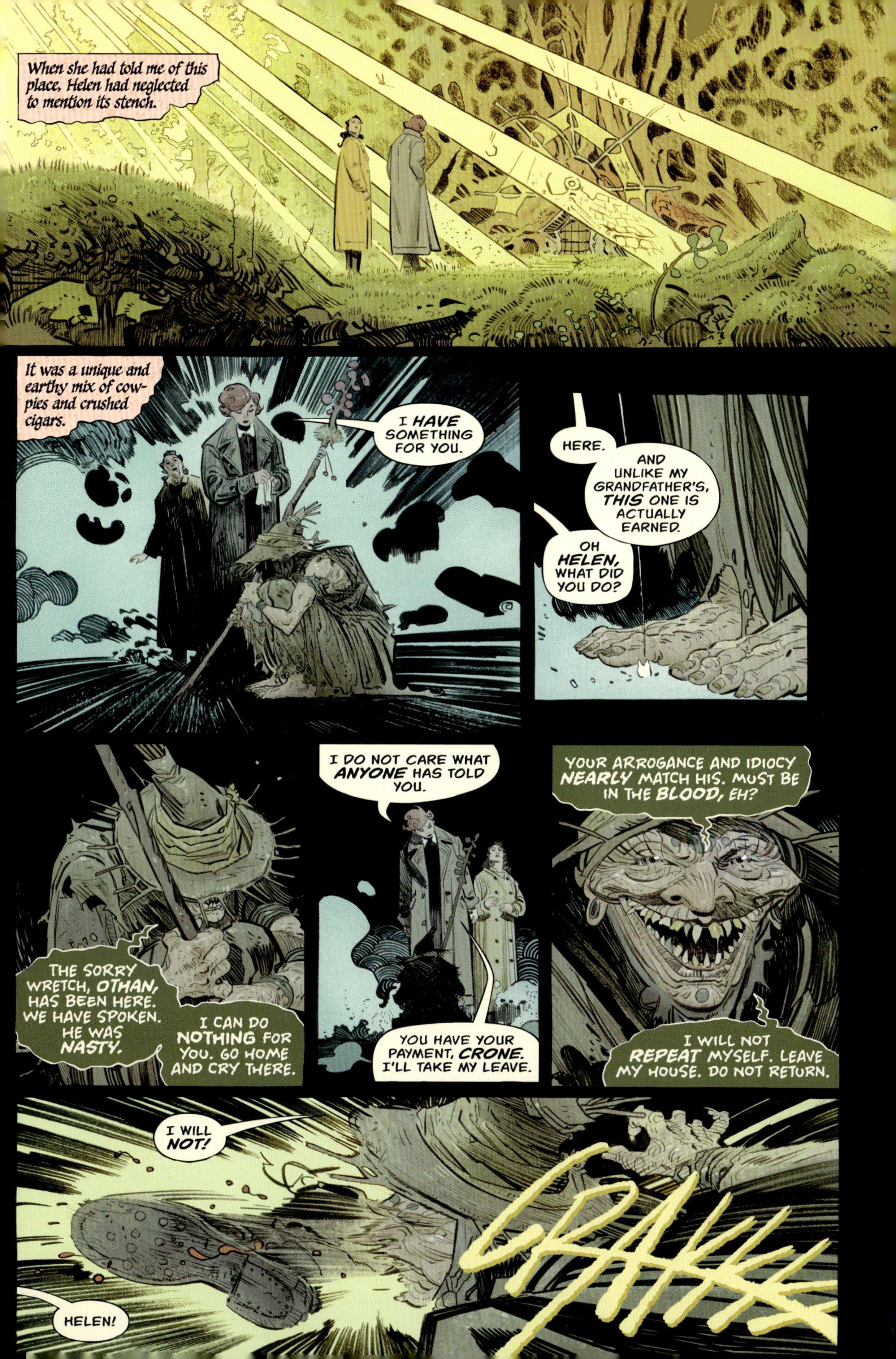
When she had told me of this place, Helen had neglected to mention its stench.
It was a unique and earthy mix of cow-pies and crushed cigars.
I HAVE SOMETHING FOR YOU.
HERE.
AND UNLIKE MY GRANDFATHER'S, THIS ONE IS ACTUALLY EARNED.
OH HELEN, WHAT DID YOU DO?
THE SORRY WRETCH, OTHAN, HAS BEEN HERE. WE HAVE SPOKEN. HE WAS NASTY.
I CAN DO NOTHING FOR YOU. GO HOME AND CRY THERE.
I DO NOT CARE WHAT ANYONE HAS TOLD YOU.
YOU HAVE YOUR PAYMENT, CRONE. I'LL TAKE MY LEAVE.
YOUR ARROGANCE AND IDIOCY NEARLY MATCH HIS. MUST BE IN THE BLOOD, EH?
I WILL NOT REPEAT MYSELF. LEAVE MY HOUSE. DO NOT RETURN.
I WILL NOT!
CRAKK
HELEN!

HOW DARE YOU...
JUST CHOMP ON THOSE AGAIN AND COUNT IT AS A TIP FROM ME TO YOU.
AND WE'LL BE ON OUR WAY INTO THE DESERT.
AAAAAH!!!
I REMEMBER READING ABOUT YOU, CRONE. IN THE ELEPHANT'S TALE BY C.K. COLE.
I WAS LITTLE AND I THOUGHT YOU WERE SO INCREDIBLY SCARY. WITH YOUR CURVED NAILS AND THE SCREECHING OF YOUR VOICE.
I HID THE PULP UNDER MY BED AFTER I WAS DONE.
BUT YOU KNOW, I STILL COULDN'T SLEEP. SO I WOKE UP DADDY AND I TOLD HIM TO TAKE YOU OUT OF THE STORY.
BUT HE NEVER LISTENED TO ME. HE WAS SO STUBBORN.
SNAPPP
SO YES, MAYBE IT IS IN THE BLOOD.

This was my first time seeing anyone killed in front of me. I wanted to vomit.
HELEN, WHAT DID YOU DO?
Later, in the war, death would become the everyday.
IT'S HER FAULT.
And each time I witnessed its obdurate depravities, I would remember that cabin.
SHE'S DEAD. DEAR LORD IN HEAVEN.
All Helen thought she might accomplish through violence and murder.
I PAID HER. SHE SHOULD'VE DONE WHAT SHE WAS SUPPOSED TO DO. EVERYONE HAS A PURPOSE.
IF YOU DON'T HAVE PURPOSE, WHAT ARE YOU THEN? JUST A BODY ON THE FLOOR.
And yet we remained deep in the forest far from any other world.
NO...

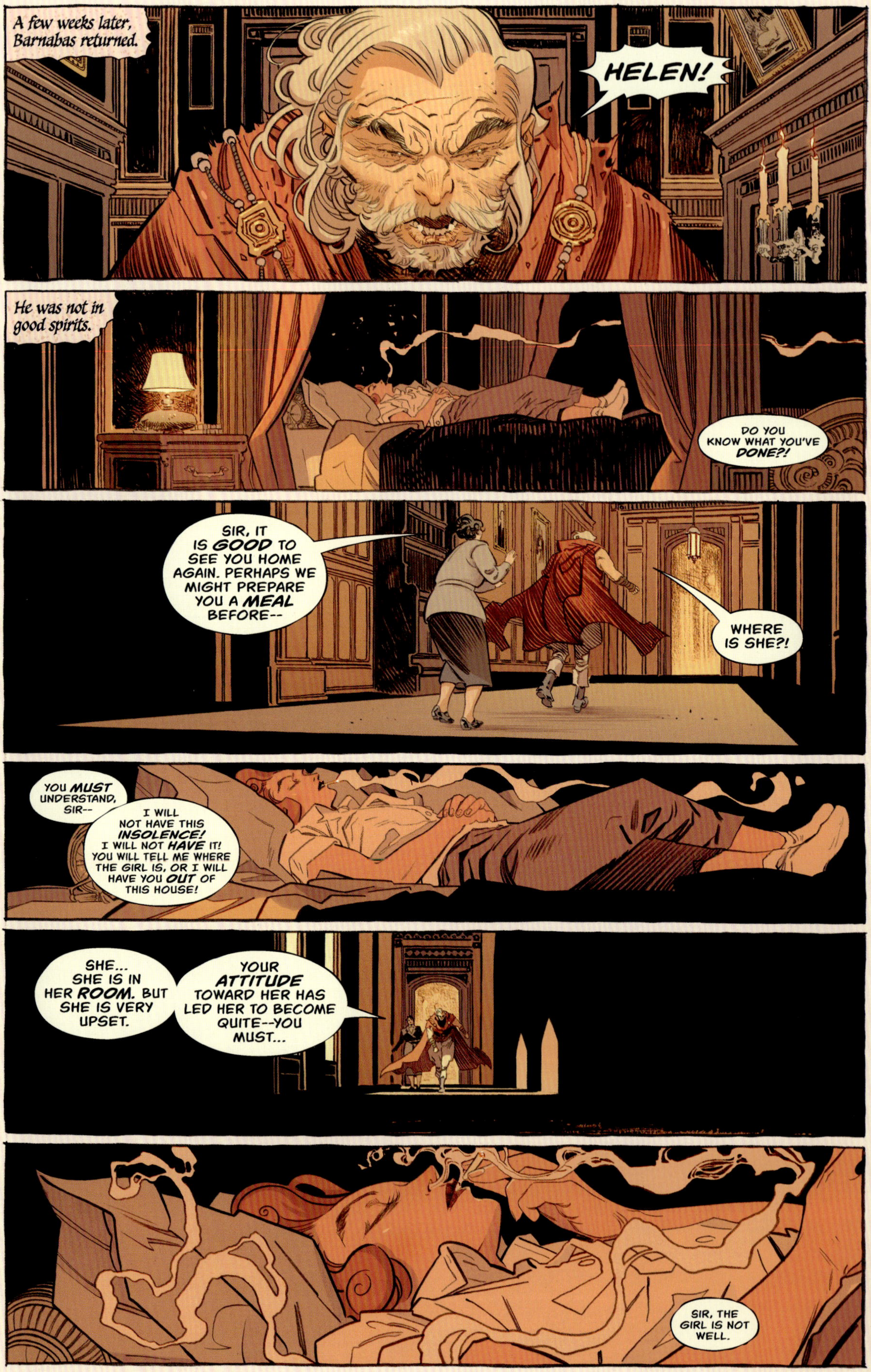
A few weeks later, Barnabas returned.
HELEN!
He was not in good spirits.
DO YOU KNOW WHAT YOU'VE DONE?!
SIR, IT IS GOOD TO SEE YOU HOME AGAIN. PERHAPS WE MIGHT PREPARE YOU A MEAL BEFORE--
WHERE IS SHE?!
YOU MUST UNDERSTAND, SIR--
I WILL NOT HAVE THIS INSOLENCE! I WILL NOT HAVE IT! YOU WILL TELL ME WHERE THE GIRL IS, OR I WILL HAVE YOU OUT OF THIS HOUSE!
SHE... SHE IS IN HER ROOM. BUT SHE IS VERY UPSET.
YOUR ATTITUDE TOWARD HER HAS LED HER TO BECOME QUITE--YOU MUST...
SIR, THE GIRL IS NOT WELL.

He ordered me to stay put. Nonetheless, I followed him up to her room, but held back in the hallway where he could not see me.
So what I tell you next is based only on what I heard from around the corner.
BANG BANG
YOU WILL OPEN THIS DOOR, WOMAN! NOW!
DO YOU HAVE ANY IDEA WHAT HELL YOU PUT ME THROUGH?! THE CRONE CROSSING IS NOT EASILY REPLACED!
I HAD TO SET SAIL ON THE THIRTEEN SEAS! WITH THAT INTOLERABLE CAPTAIN MGORGE! ALL HIS TALK OF HIS GREAT TIGER ARMY!
I HAVE AVOIDED THAT MAN FOR FIFTY YEARS!
AND THEN I HAD TO TREK THROUGH THE HEART OF THE EASTERN FROST STORMS!
I LOST THREE TOES TO THE BLUE BITE!
GO AWAY.
YOU HAD NO RIGHT TO TOUCH THAT WOMAN!
SHE IS ONE OF THE SIX KEYS TO THE--
THIS IS YOUR HOUSE. FINE. BUT IT'S MY ROOM.
AND I DON'T LIKE YOU BANGING ON MY DOOR. IT GIVES ME A HEADACHE.
JUST LEAVE. PLEASE.

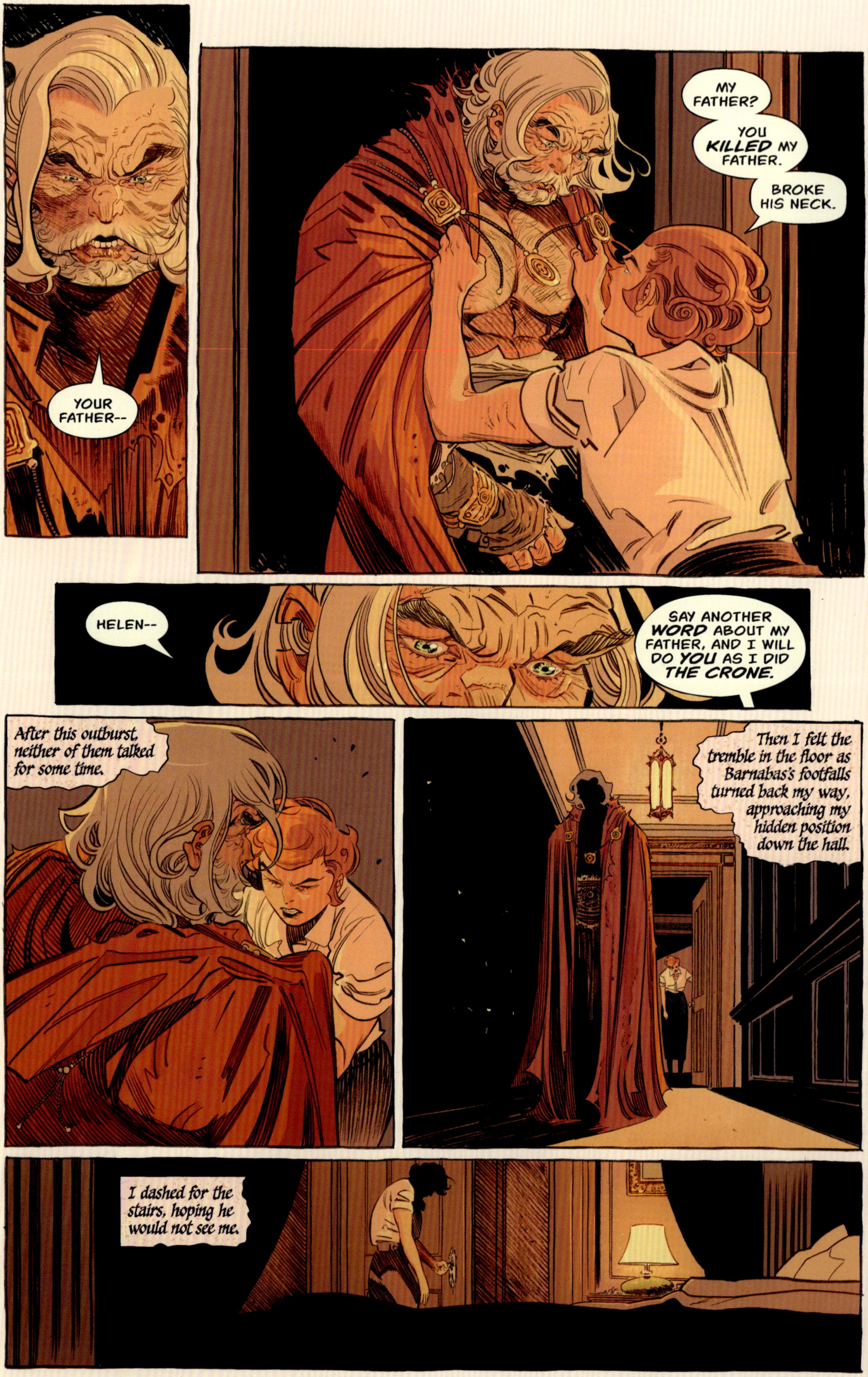

YOUR FATHER--
MY FATHER?
YOU KILLED MY FATHER.
BROKE HIS NECK.
HELEN--
SAY ANOTHER WORD ABOUT MY FATHER, AND I WILL DO YOU AS I DID THE CRONE.
After this outburst, neither of them talked for some time.
Then I felt the tremble in the floor as Barnabas's footfalls turned back my way, approaching my hidden position down the hall.
I dashed for the stairs, hoping he would not see me.

That night, Helen did not come to my room.
I tried to sleep but instead spent my moments turning from one side to the other.
In the small hours of the night, I noticed a light coming from my window.
It seemed as if something in the garden was aglow, perhaps on fire.
I went down to investigate and found Helen and the fairies.

I WAS LOOKING FOR SOMETHING IN THE SHED, AND THERE WAS A SACK JUST LYING THERE.
I OPENED IT AND LOOK WHAT CAME OUT.
BARNABAS MUST HAVE BROUGHT THEM BACK WITH HIM.
AH. YES. BUT HELEN, IT'S VERY LATE.
WHATEVER WERE YOU LOOKING FOR IN THE SHED AT THIS HOUR?
UHM, A ROPE.
TO HANG MYSELF.
HELEN!
NO!

YOU SCARED THEM.
THEY DON'T LIKE LOUD NOISES, DO THEY?
WHAT IS THIS GOBBLEDYGOOK ABOUT A ROPE AND... AND...SELF-HARM?!
I WILL NOT HEAR THAT! NO.
I THOUGHT TO USE A BELT LIKE HE DID.
BUT THEN I REMEMBER DAD WRITING, ALWAYS GOING ON ABOUT BEING ORIGINAL, IMAGINING SOMETHING DIFFERENT AND NEW AND STRANGE AND WEIRD.
SO I WENT TO GET A ROPE INSTEAD. NOT GREAT, BUT...I'M NOT THAT GREAT, SO IT'LL DO.
HELEN, I DID NOT KNOW YOUR FATHER, BUT FROM YOUR OWN DESCRIPTIONS I IMAGINE HIM TO BE AN HONORABLE IF, AT TIMES, FLAWED MAN.
AND I AM SURE, AS I AM SURE OF ANYTHING, THAT THE LAST THING HE WOULD'VE WANTED IS FOR YOU TO GO DOWN THIS UNFORTUNATE PATH.
IT IS UNGODLY.
MY FATHER DIDN'T BELIEVE IN GOD. AND NEITHER DO I.
BUT BOTH OF US BELIEVED IN FAIRIES.
AND NOW THEY TOO HAVE LEFT ME.

HELEN, MY DEAR, IS IT ALL THAT BAD?
DADDY WAS SCARED ALL THE TIME. I COULD ALWAYS SEE IT. BUT HE TRIED TO HIDE IT. BUT IT WAS THERE, AT EVERY BAR AND HOTEL. THERE WAS A TREMBLE TO HIM.
AND I THINK HE WAS SO SCARED, HE DID THAT WITH HIS BELT, JUST TO STOP THE SHAKE. AND I DON'T EVEN KNOW WHAT HE WAS SCARED OF.
AND I THINK, IF I GET SCARED, I HAVE TO DO IT TOO. WE JUST--YOUR PARENTS--YOU JUST RUN WHERE THEY WERE RUNNING.
HELEN, PLEASE.
IT'S ALL RIGHT, DEAR.
WHEN I WAS OVER THERE WITH GRANDPA, AND I HAD MY STEEL AND THERE WERE DEMONS ALL ABOUT AND DESTRUCTION WAS JUST A BREATH AWAY...
...I WASN'T SCARED AT ALL. I KNEW, IN THE DEEP HEART OF ME, THAT I WASN'T LIKE MY FATHER. I WAS BRAVE AND I WOULDN'T HAVE TO RUN AT ALL.
AND THEN... THEN...
...IT'S ALL JUST GONE, AND WHAT AM I NOW?
A GIRL IN A GARDEN. TREMBLING.
I'M SO SCARED.
I CAN'T STOP IT.

I took her back to the manor and saw her to sleep in my bed.
I woke before dawn, and, with Helen still resting soundly, I set off to find the master of the house.
I could not locate him in his bedroom or office. In desperation I sought out Joseph, who was then cleaning the kitchen.
SMAK
Joseph informed me in his typical condescending tone that Barnabas had left a few hours earlier. Off to the other world for possibly months.
Realizing the danger in this outcome, I demanded to know by what route he was traveling, given that the Crone was now dead.
Joseph took in my desperation, hesitated, and then laughed heartily.
"To the east," he said. "There is a creek that runs through the trees. Those who walk its path at times get where they're going.
"But mostly they just drown."

And the second time that season...
BARNABAS!
...I chased a Cole of Wyndhorn House to the edge of the world.
WHAT MADNESS IS THIS?
WOULD YOU PLEASE SLOW DOWN, SIR?!
I AM DRENCHED AND UNCOMFORTABLE AND EXHAUSTED.
AND I NEED TO TALK WITH YOU.

THIS IS NOT A PLACE FOR GOVERNESSES, WOMAN.
GO BACK TO WYNDHORN.
I WILL DO NO SUCH THING.
NOT UNTIL YOU HEAR OF THE GREAT DAMAGE YOU HAVE DONE.
I HAVE NO TIME FOR FOOLISHNESS.
THERE ARE HORRORS IN THESE WATERS. THEY KNOW MY SKILL AND KEEP THEIR DISTANCE.
BUT YOUR UNFAMILIAR FLESH WILL SOON DRAW THEIR HUNGER AND OVERCOME THAT SMALL INSTINCT OF FRIGHT.
THE ONLY HORROR I SEE AROUND HERE IS YOU.
THE WAY YOU TREAT THAT GIRL, YOUR OWN GRANDDAUGHTER. IT IS DREADFUL WHAT YOU HAVE DONE. CAN YOU NOT SEE THAT?
NO...
DAMMIT, WOMAN. DO YOU EVER LISTEN?
NOW IT IS TOO LATE.
DO I EVER LISTEN? ALL I DO IS SIT AROUND LISTENING!
BUT IT IS TIME I LET MY VOICE BE HEARD AMONG YOUR CACOPHONY OF ABSURDITIES!
I HATE TO SAY THIS TO YOU, AS YOU ARE MY EMPLOYER, BUT IT MUST BE UTTERED...

Now, I should say, what came next was rather unexpected.
YOU ARE A FOOL, BARNABAS COLE!
FROM THE HAIR ON YOUR HEAD TO THE SOLES OF YOUR FEET! A FOOL, THROUGH AND THROUGH!
GRRAGGG!

I am not speaking, as you might suppose, of the towering monster that arose from what seemed to clearly be a fairly shallow and cold creek bed.
CAN YOU NOT SEE DEATH IS HERE, WOMAN?! MOVE!
OH!
What was truly a shock to me at that time was not its jagged teeth, or its horrid yawp, or its obvious desire for our blood and bones.
SIR! HOW DARE YOU!
DESPITE MY STATION, I AM NOT TO BE TOSSED LIKE A STICK IN A FIELD!
No, what was more surprising than all that worry was how little I cared that a monster was there.
IF YOU MUST USE WORDS, USE THEM FOR PRAYER.
ONLY THE GODS MAY SAVE US NOW.
I SEE YOU'VE GOT YOURSELF ANOTHER DISTRACTION! HOW SPLENDID AND NOBLE!
MEANWHILE, THAT POOR GIRL IS AT HOME IN TEARS, NOT KNOWING IF SHE IS COMING OR GOING!
DOES THIS REALLY SATISFY YOU?!
YOU HAVE BROUGHT DOOM UPON US BOTH AND YOU CONTINUE!
DO YOU EVER KEEP QUIET, WOMAN?!
WHEN IT COMES TO THE CARE OF MY CHARGE?
NO, SIR, I DO NOT.

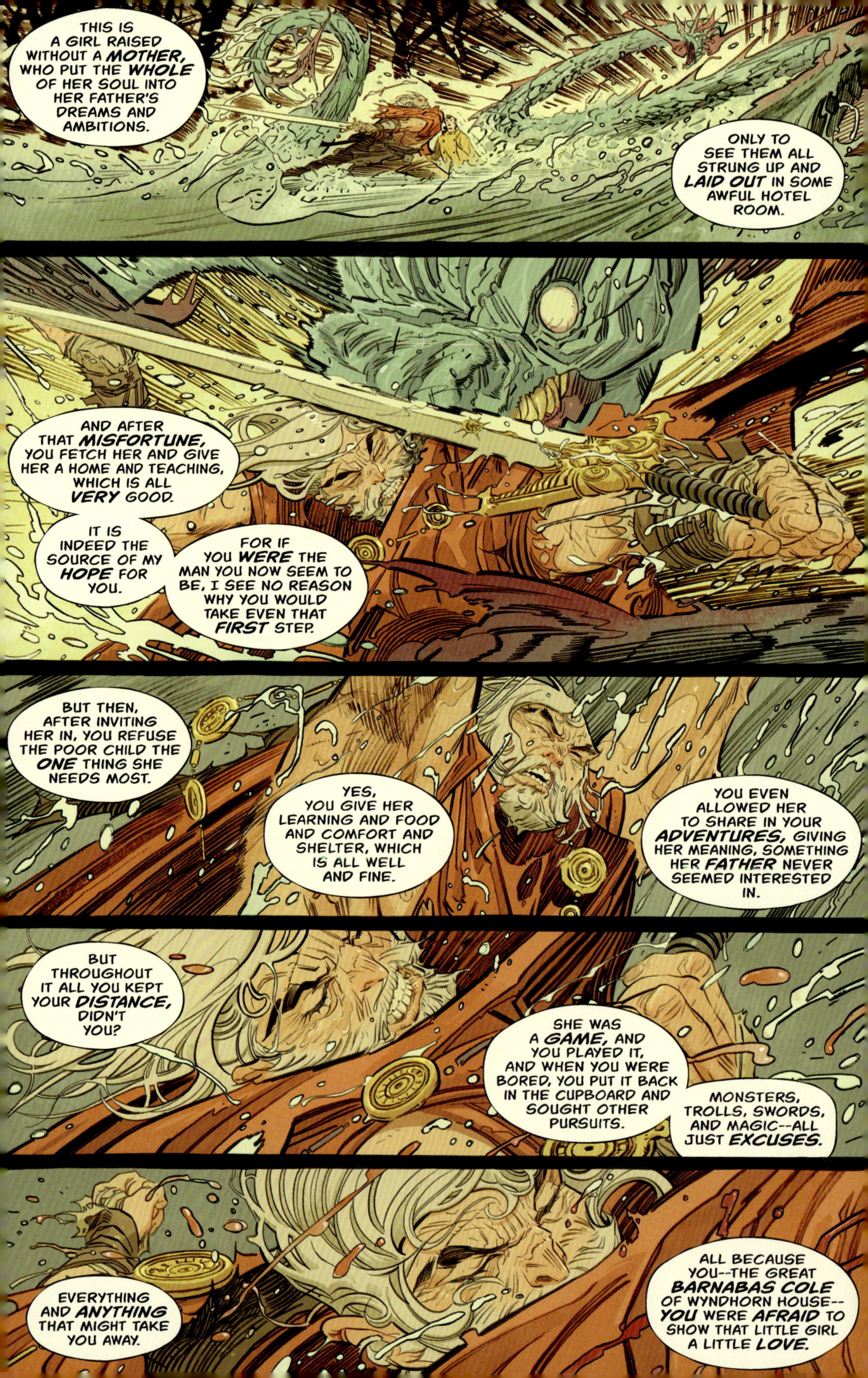

THIS IS A GIRL RAISED WITHOUT A MOTHER, WHO PUT THE WHOLE OF HER SOUL INTO HER FATHER'S DREAMS AND AMBITIONS.
ONLY TO SEE THEM ALL STRUNG UP AND LAID OUT IN SOME AWFUL HOTEL ROOM.
AND AFTER THAT MISFORTUNE, YOU FETCH HER AND GIVE HER A HOME AND TEACHING, WHICH IS ALL VERY GOOD.
IT IS INDEED THE SOURCE OF MY HOPE FOR YOU.
FOR IF YOU WERE THE MAN YOU NOW SEEM TO BE, I SEE NO REASON WHY YOU WOULD TAKE EVEN THAT FIRST STEP.
BUT THEN, AFTER INVITING HER IN, YOU REFUSE THE POOR CHILD THE ONE THING SHE NEEDS MOST.
YES, YOU GIVE HER LEARNING AND FOOD AND COMFORT AND SHELTER, WHICH IS ALL WELL AND FINE.
YOU EVEN ALLOWED HER TO SHARE IN YOUR ADVENTURES, GIVING HER MEANING, SOMETHING HER FATHER NEVER SEEMED INTERESTED IN.
BUT THROUGHOUT IT ALL YOU KEPT YOUR DISTANCE, DIDN'T YOU?
SHE WAS A GAME, AND YOU PLAYED IT, AND WHEN YOU WERE BORED, YOU PUT IT BACK IN THE CUPBOARD AND SOUGHT OTHER PURSUITS.
MONSTERS, TROLLS, SWORDS, AND MAGIC--ALL JUST EXCUSES.
EVERYTHING AND ANYTHING THAT MIGHT TAKE YOU AWAY.
ALL BECAUSE YOU--THE GREAT BARNABAS COLE OF WYNDHORN HOUSE--YOU WERE AFRAID TO SHOW THAT LITTLE GIRL A LITTLE LOVE.

SHE IS **DYING**, BARNABAS. LIKE HER FATHER BEFORE HER.
AAAAAAAAAH!
YOU COULD **NOT** SAVE HIM. I DO NOT KNOW WHY.
THAT IS BETWEEN YOURSELF, YOUR SON, AND GOD.
BUT YOU **CAN** SAVE HER.
I KNOW THAT AS SURELY AS I KNOW ONE AND ONE ARE TWO.
AND BECAUSE I KNOW, IT'S **NOT** JUST BETWEEN YOURSELF, HELEN, AND OUR **LORD**.
NO.
I AM HERE TOO.

As was his way, he did not say much after that.
He checked his kill, looked at me, then nodded ever so slightly. And though I would not swear to it, I do believe I saw tears in his eyes.
Then he turned from me and walked back toward Wyndhorn.
Without a further word, I followed after him, keeping pace through the creek.
And so we journeyed home, leaving the monster behind.
GARAGE SALE

CHAPTER VI

THERE, YOU SEE?!
DESPITE ALL YOUR PERNICIOUS LITTLE DOUBTS AND COMPLAINTS!
ONCE AGAIN, MY HAIRY FRIEND, I HAVE GUIDED YOU THROUGH THE STORM!
THE LAND IS HERE! THE SUN IS SHINING!
SOON, ALL WILL BE WELL!

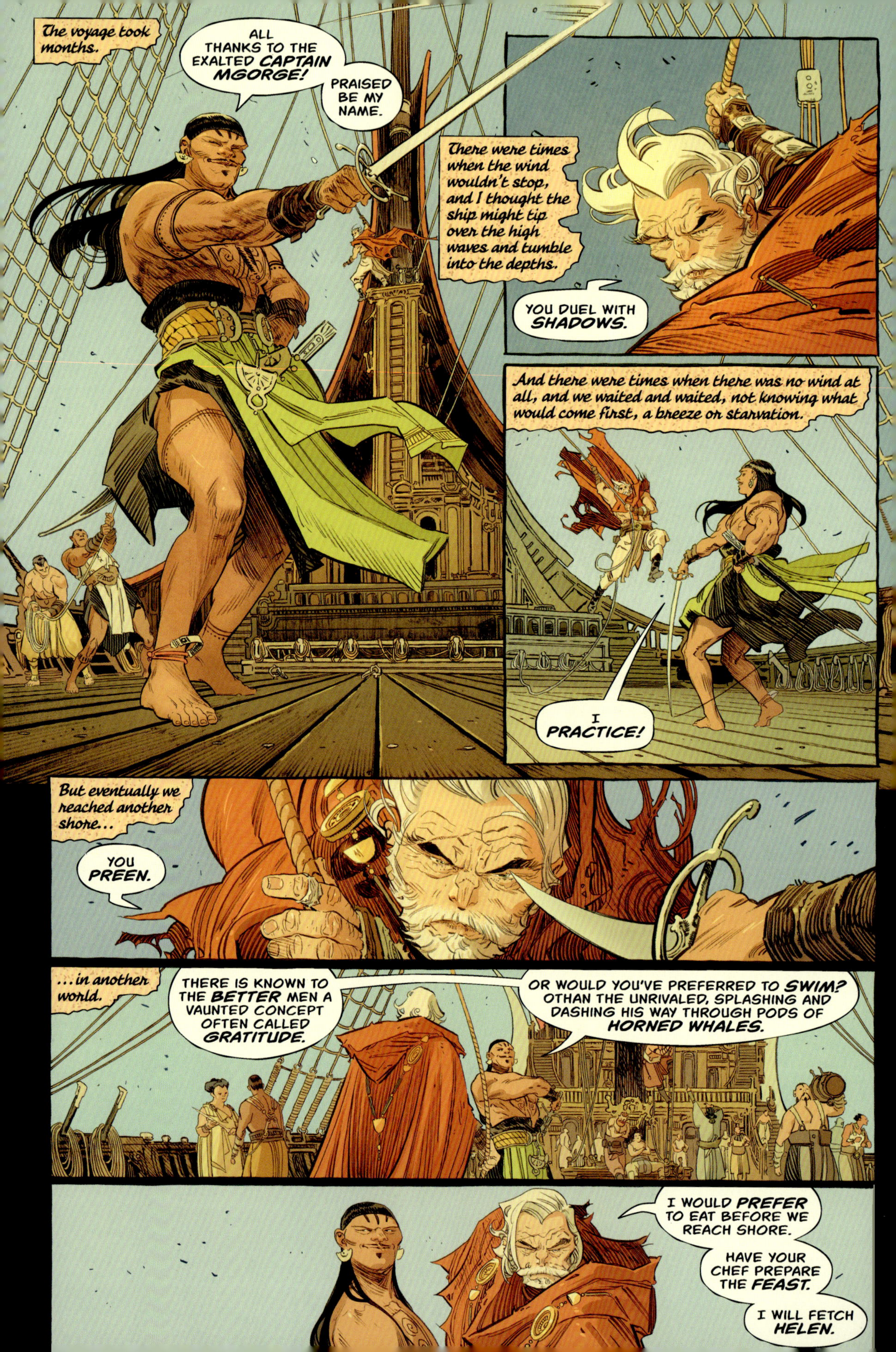
The voyage took months.
ALL THANKS TO THE EXALTED CAPTAIN MGORGE!
PRAISED BE MY NAME.
There were times when the wind wouldn't stop, and I thought the ship might tip over the high waves and tumble into the depths.
YOU DUEL WITH SHADOWS.
And there were times when there was no wind at all, and we waited and waited, not knowing what would come first, a breeze or starvation.
I PRACTICE!
But eventually we reached another shore...
YOU PREEN.
...in another world.
THERE IS KNOWN TO THE BETTER MEN A VAUNTED CONCEPT OFTEN CALLED GRATITUDE.
OR WOULD YOU'VE PREFERRED TO SWIM? OTHAN THE UNRIVALED, SPLASHING AND DASHING HIS WAY THROUGH PODS OF HORNED WHALES.
I WOULD PREFER TO EAT BEFORE WE REACH SHORE.
HAVE YOUR CHEF PREPARE THE FEAST.
I WILL FETCH HELEN.

AH, 'TIS A PITY TO LOSE YOU, BEAUTIFUL. WE COULD NOT HAVE SURVIVED THE BLOOD RAINS IF IT WERE NOT FOR YOUR STEEL.
IN THE SEA, THE STARS ARE MY GUIDE, AND WHEN THE CLOUDS ROLL OVER US AND THEIR SHINE SADLY FADES, I AM LOST.
HOW I MISS THEIR SHINE IS HOW I WILL NOW MISS YOU.
IT IS NOT TIME FOR YOUR CARPING, CAPTAIN.
MOVE AND LET THE GIRL BOARD.
I REGRET TO LEAVE YOU IN SUCH BOORISH COMPANY, DEAR, BUT IT SEEMS TIME AND TIDE AND GRANDFATHER ALL SHARE A LACK OF PATIENCE.
HOW YOUR GRACE DESCENDED FROM HIS DROSS REMAINS A PUZZLE I WILL PONDER EVEN AS MY SOUL SHEDS ITS SKIN.
I HOPE YOU CAN FORGIVE ME FOR NOT BRINGING YOU THE REST OF THE WAY!
BUT THE COVE OF CASTRATA IS NOT KIND TO OUR KIND, AND I ENJOY BREATHING THE SALT SEA A TAD TOO MUCH TO GIVE IT UP AT THIS EARLY DATE!
REGARDLESS, GOOD FORTUNE, MY FRIENDS!
MAY YOUR DEATHS BE HONORABLE AND QUICK!

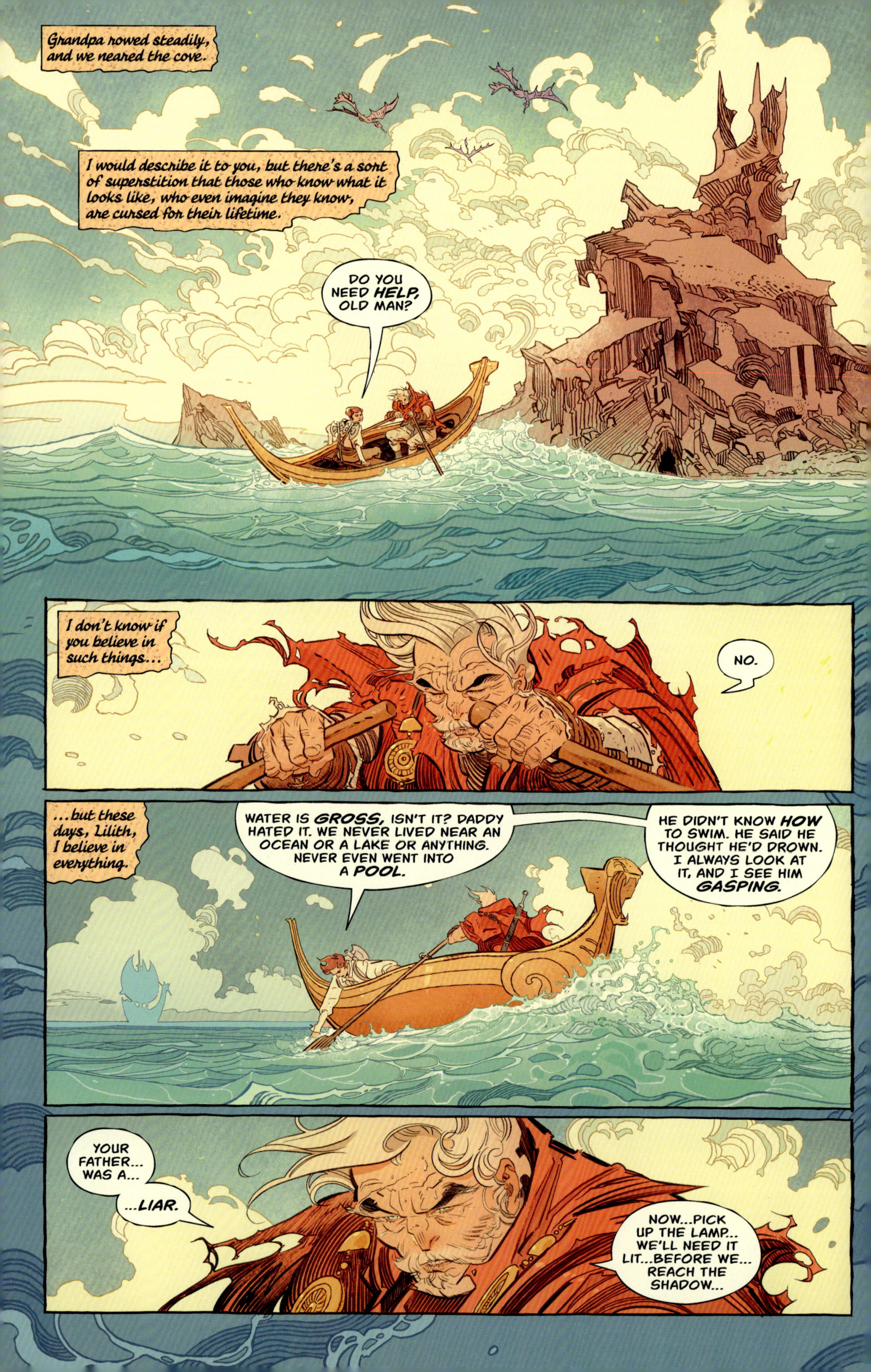
Grandpa rowed steadily, and we neared the cove.
I would describe it to you, but there's a sort of superstition that those who know what it looks like, who even imagine they know, are cursed for their lifetime.
DO YOU NEED HELP, OLD MAN?
I don't know if you believe in such things...
NO.
...but these days, Lilith, I believe in everything.
WATER IS GROSS, ISN'T IT? DADDY HATED IT. WE NEVER LIVED NEAR AN OCEAN OR A LAKE OR ANYTHING. NEVER EVEN WENT INTO A POOL.
HE DIDN'T KNOW HOW TO SWIM. HE SAID HE THOUGHT HE'D DROWN. I ALWAYS LOOK AT IT, AND I SEE HIM GASPING.
YOUR FATHER... WAS A...
...LIAR.
NOW...PICK UP THE LAMP... WE'LL NEED IT LIT...BEFORE WE... REACH THE SHADOW...

We entered the cove and darkness consumed us. Only the small lantern provided any illumination to the mysteries ahead.
DO YOU THINK I WAS BORN FOR YOU, OTHAN?
THERE ARE OTHERS IN THE WORLD, YOU KNOW. THEIR TIME ALSO MATTERS.
The voice was familiar, but the light would not reach her, though I swear we were close enough.
WHO...?
THE CRONE IS DEAD. MGORGE SAILS LIKE A TODDLER TESTING HIS FIRST STEPS.
I AM NOT LATE BY CHOICE.
I could just make out her figure standing in the middle of the water. And just that was enough for a feeling of intimidation and warmth to cover me.
YOU FOREVER DEFINE YOURSELF BY YOUR EXCUSES, AND APPALLINGLY YOU THINK IT ENDEARING.
COME NOW, LET'S HAVE IT OVER WITH.
And from the slight tremble in my grandfather's typically stolid voice, I understood he too felt her power.
YES. WELL. BE UNDER NO ILLUSIONS.
MY ENJOYMENT IN THIS FARCE IS NO GREATER THAN YOURS.
YOU RETURNED THE FLYUNE.
A DEBT IS TO BE PAID.
AND THAT IS ALL.

As their lips met, a sharp light burst beneath them.
And I knew her.
I had met her on a hilltop the first time I traveled to the Other World.
She took my breath then. She took it again here.
She was the Hearth.
My grandmother.

The light continued to build, until I was blinded by it.
For a moment, all was the shine of her kiss.
Then the glare dimmed. And she was gone.
DOES SHE--
INTO THE WATER NOW. SWIM DOWN. HARD AS YOU CAN. DO NOT STOP.
AND QUICKLY. BEFORE THE LIGHT FADES ENTIRELY.
WE DO NOT NEED TO FACE THE UNDERS IN THEIR INK.
NO, I TOLD YOU. MY DAD... WE DIDN'T... EVER...
I...
I DON'T KNOW HOW TO SWIM.
YES, HELEN.
YOU MOST CERTAINLY DO.

He dove in, gliding like a young shark, heading straight toward the unseen bottom fathoms below.
I waited for him to return.
Surely he needed to come up soon to catch a breath, and then I could tell him again, convince him, that I couldn't do this.
I just needed to be patient, and he'd come, and he would see how scared I was, and we'd go another way.
He'd see. He had to. I was so afraid.
I could show him how afraid I was. Just like...
AND THEN, IN THE MIDDLE OF THAT CAVE, IN THE MIDDLE OF MY MIND, I SAW MY FATHER, SAW HIM LAUGHING, LOUD AND LONG.
LILITH, YOU DON'T UNDERSTAND, I SAW HIM.
AND HE HAD SUCH A BEAUTIFUL LAUGH.
I found myself diving into the water.
Because I suddenly knew two things to be true.
My grandfather was not returning.
And I was no longer afraid.

To my shock, I was good at it.
It all seemed very natural. As simple as having a heartbeat.
Something you just always have done and hopefully always will do.
It was so effortless that I soon found myself by Grandpa's side though he had left the surface well before I had.
I was trying to understand this strangeness, when the next oddity came crashing down upon me.
Because that's when, underwater, leagues under water, Barnabas-- Lilith, he started to talk.
And I could hear him as if he was here sitting with me on this bed.
DON'T GO TOO FAR PAST ME.
THEY'RE IDIOTS, AND THEY WON'T KNOW YOU, AND THEY DON'T LIKE OUTSIDERS.
And without thinking, I responded.
ALL RIGHT.
At which point it occurred to me that I was still breathing.
WHAT IS THIS--
But before I could understand that insanity, the Unders were upon us.

I had some experience. I had seen Barnabas hold off dragons.
And though underwater men were not my every-day, I did not doubt they too would fall before him.
YOU IMBECILES, DO YOU KNOW--
But, as you may have gathered, it was a day of astonishments.
GUHHH!
Enough that I was distracted and stupidly did not see the swift crowd forming around me.
Before I could even reach for an axe, they had my hands pinned.
I expected Barnabas to lash out with his sword and to be awash in a sea of blood.
Instead, he used his tongue.
DO YOU WANT TO DIE?!
DO YOU NOT SEE WHO SHE IS?! LOOK AT HER, YOU DAMN BEAR FOOD!
For the life of me I could not fathom what good that would do.
THAT IS HELEN OF WYNDHORN.
But words are uncanny things and sometimes carry strange powers.
DAUGHTER OF YOUR WITCH OF THE WAVES.

And with nothing more than that, they released their grips and backed away, their many eyes fixed upon me.
All of them anticipating something. What, I could not guess.
WE ARE HERE FOR MEMORIAM. AS IS HER RIGHT, AS IS HER DUTY.
WE WILL HAVE STEEDS AND AN ESCORT TO THE EDGE.
AND WE WILL HAVE THEM SWIFTLY.
As fast as they arrived, they left even faster.
Scattering into the endless sea and soon disappearing beyond our sight.
WITCH OF THE WAVES?
THE UNDERS HAVE THEIR MYTHS LIKE ANYONE ELSE.
IT'S ALL BLATHER. THE UNIVERSE IS A LOBSTER TAIL UPON WHICH THE GODS GNAW. I DON'T KNOW.
EVEN YOUR FATHER WOULD MOCK IT.
STEEDS?

I used to spend my days waking up hung over, waking my hung-over father, nagging at him, getting him to write a few pages.
Then we'd go down to the bank, cash whatever latest check had come from whatever cheap pulp had agreed to publish him.
And we'd spend the rest of the afternoon and night drinking away the money, promising ourselves that we'd save some pennies to stave off our debts.
Eventually we'd wander home on unsteady legs and pass out, knowing we'd have to run from the creditors in the morning.
That day, Lilith, far beneath the waves, accompanied by the Unders and Othan the Brutal, I rode to the Long Edge of the Deep.
On a horned whale.

A few hours later, we arrived.
ARE THEY COMING WITH US?
NO.
THEY'RE PETRIFIED OF THEIR OWN GOD. IDIOTS.
I'LL USE THESE, YOU USE YOUR AXES.
DON'T LET GO OF THE CLIFF. THERE ARE CURRENTS HERE THAT WILL PULL YOU INTO THE DEEP.
I CANNOT RESCUE YOU THERE.
HOW FAR DOES IT GO?
FAR.

Down and down we went.
SHOULDN'T WE BE DEAD?
THE KISS. THE HEARTH PROTECTS ME.
Hours, days, I don't know.
WELL, BULLY FOR YOU.
WHAT ABOUT ME?
YOU'RE FINE.
We descended from all we knew.
WHAT IF I'M NOT FINE?
YOU'RE FINE.

Finally, we reached the bottom.
As you well know, Lilith, Grandfather prefers deeds to speech. He rarely will answer a direct question with more than a grunt.
But then, as we walked past the flames, he just... he just started talking.
THE LAST TIME I WAS HERE, I WAS WITH YOUR FATHER.
I WOULD NOT HAVE COME. I HATE IT HERE. BUT HE ASKED ME.
HE WAS NOT A CHILD WHO ASKED FOR MUCH.
BUT HE COULD NOT FACE THIS ALONE, HE SAID. I COULD SEE FEAR IN HIM.
HE WAS ALSO NOT A CHILD WHO FEARED MUCH.
AND SO HIS MOTHER LENT US SOME OF HER SPIRIT, AS SHE HAS DONE FOR ME THIS DAY, AND WE HEADED DOWN.
TO SEE HIS WIFE DIE.
AND TO TAKE HIS DAUGHTER HOME.

I'm useless, Lilith. Daddy would've written something spare but perfect.
You could've seen it all in your mind's eye.
I never knew her. I'd never seen a picture of her. Daddy didn't talk about her. He said she was just a girl in a bar. Just someone to be forgotten.
And there.
Daddy would've done it right, all the adjectives twisting their nouns into perfection, and then he would have sold it for a bottle of whisky.
WHY?
But me?
YOUR GOVERNESS. SHE HAS INFORMED ME THAT YOU...
...THAT YOU WERE SUFFERING. AS MY BOY ONCE SUFFERED.
I have no words.
HE AND I. WE. WE...
...WE FLED FROM OUR PAIN.
WITH... WITH YOU... I WOULD...
HELEN, WE SHOULD PERHAPS NOT FLEE.
FROM ONE ANOTHER.

We spent some time in the cathedral with Mother.
THE SWORD ROOM. JOSEPH SAYS YOU COLLECTED ALL THOSE THOUSANDS OF SWORDS AND YOU JUST PUT THEM IN THERE.
YOU DON'T SEEM LIKE SOMEONE WHO COLLECTS THINGS.
It was quiet, and she was beautiful.
JOSEPH.
I COULD TELL YOU STORIES ABOUT THAT MAN.
Then we returned to land.
IT'S DAD'S SWORD. YOU MUST HAVE GIVEN HIM ONE. AND...WHEN HE LEFT. WITH ME. HE SOLD IT. PROBABLY TO GET MONEY FOR ME TO EAT. THAT'S WHAT HE WOULD DO.
AND YOU...YOU'RE LOOKING FOR IT.
Mgorge would be back with his ship the next day...
JOSEPH SHOULD KEEP HIS MOUTH SHUT.
...leaving us hours to sit on the beach.
WILL YOU TELL ME ABOUT MOTHER AND FATHER?
I DIDN'T KNOW THEM.
I couldn't think of what to say to him.
I AM NO BARD.
"Thank you" or "damn you."
NO, NOT YOU, GRANDPA. YOU'RE A SAVAGE WARRIOR WHO SEEKS TREASURE. WHO TRADES FOR IT.
SO HOW ABOUT THIS? LET'S TRADE. TREASURE FOR STORIES.
Both or neither.
TREASURE? HEH.
WHAT DO YOU HAVE THAT IS OF ANY WORTH TO ME?
I don't know if I did it right.
YOU TELL ME ABOUT MY FATHER BEFORE HE LEFT. WHEN HE WAS WITH YOU.
AND I WILL TELL YOU ABOUT HIM AFTER. WHEN HE TOOK CARE OF ME.

He sat for some time with that.
HM.
When he talked, he spoke slowly, haltingly.
YOUR...
YOUR FATHER...
But he did talk.
YOUR FATHER WAS AN **OBNOXIOUS** CHILD.
JOSEPH WOULD CHASE HIM AROUND **WYNDHORN,** ONE ROOM AFTER ANOTHER, **SCOLDING** HIM FOR WHATEVER WAS HIS LATEST SIN.
EVENTUALLY, THE BOY WOULD **DASH** INTO MY STUDY AND HIDE BEHIND ME, **BEGGING** MY FORGIVENESS, SEEKING MY AID.
WHEN JOSEPH FOLLOWED INTO THE ROOM, I SAID MY SON HAD TAKEN AN **INVISIBILITY** POTION AND I COULD NOT SEE HIM.
JOSEPH WOULD SCOWL AND C.K. AND I WOULD LAUGH AS I LOOKED EVERYWHERE FOR HIM, BUT NEVER **SAW** HIM...

Helen did not tell me any more of their travels or shared stories, not that day at least.
She simply noted that the rest of the trip was uneventful except for a few minor skirmishes, a few dozen dead men here and there.
They returned to the house at sunset.
"It was lovely," she said. "All the colors of this world, reaching out, wrapping warmly around our home.
"Like a father holding his son for the first time."

The next day, we returned to our lessons.
AF E'S POOR PTION, HARDY DED TO DEDICAT S REST OF HIS LIFE S POETRY. THERE IS E DOUBT WHETHE S WAS A RETREAT M PUBLIC LIF AN AT T--
I HAVE A QUESTION, LILITH.
DOES IT CONCERN THOMAS HARDY?
AM I REAL?
SIGH
THAT IS CERTAINLY NOT HARDY.
PLEASE SIT. WE WILL CONTINUE.
EVERYTHING THAT'S HAPPENED SINCE FATHER DIED-- NONE OF IT MAKES ANY SENSE.
THIS WORLD, THE OTHER WORLD, I'M IN ONE OF HIS STORIES.
THERE'S SOMETHING WRONG WITH ME. I'M NOT LIKE EVERYONE ELSE, I'M BEING TOLD.

DEAR.
I AM NOT THAT MUCH OLDER THAN YOU, I GRANT YOU, BUT I HAVE PERHAPS LEARNED SOMETHING OVER THOSE FEW YEARS.
MOSTLY BECAUSE I DID NOT IGNORE MY STUDIES.
LILITH, I'M NOT TRYING TO--
WE ARE ALL THE STORY OUR PARENTS TELL.
AND WE BECOME THE STORY OUR CHILDREN, AND OUR GRANDCHILDREN, TELL.
YOU, MY DEAR, ARE NO DIFFERENT FROM ANYONE ELSE.
EXCEPT THAT YOU ARE HELEN OF WYNDHORN.
AND THAT MAKES ALL THE DIFFERENCE IN THE WORLD.

I had been in the manor now for several years and I had seen miracles and monsters that most cannot begin to comprehend.
LADIES, PARDON THE INTERRUPTION.
Yet each of these wonders were mundane next to what I witnessed that day.
JOSEPH HAS JUST INFORMED ME WAR HAS BROKEN OUT BETWEEN THE HESSITES AND THE BARBAROUS HORSEMEN.
THIS WILL LIKELY CAUSE THE GUARDS OF THE GATES TO MOVE INTO DRY VALLEY IN ORDER TO FLANK FINIAN'S LAND NAVY.
AS SUCH, THE GATES THEMSELVES WOULD BE THEN, AT LEAST SOMEWHAT, VULNERABLE TO A WELL-EXECUTED PLUNDER.
For that was the day Barnabas Cole, Othan of the Other World...
That was the day...
...AND I WAS... I HOPED... I WAS WONDERING...
...IF YOU MIGHT ACCOMPANY ME, HELEN? TO THE GATES. TO SEE.
THERE IS NO OBLIGATION. JOSEPH CAN PREPARE ANY--
...he asked for something.
NO.
YES!
HELEN COLE!
IF YOU WISH TO GO PILLAGING WITH YOUR GRANDFATHER...
...YOU MUST FINISH YOUR POETRY LESSON FIRST!

ANYWAY, IT'S GETTING LATE. I SHOULD GO.
I APPRECIATE YOU LISTENING TO AN OLD WOMAN'S REMEMBRANCES. IT DOES MAKE ONE FEEL SPECIAL, DOESN'T IT?
TELLING OLD STORIES OF LOVE AND WOE.
IS THIS A JOKE?
IS IT FUNNY?
I MEAN, IT'S STUPID. IF IT'S ALL TRUE, HOW DOES IT WORK? WAS BARNABAS BORN HERE? WHY DOES HE LIVE IN THIS WORLD AND THEN GO TO THE OTHER?
OTHAN CAN'T BE... HE'S NOT... NONE OF THIS WORKS... IT'S...
AND HOW THE HELL DOES ANY OF THIS EXPLAIN WHAT HAPPENED TO HELEN COLE?! IS SHE ACTUALLY ALIVE? IS THAT WHAT YOU'RE SAYING?
OH, WELL...
...I SUPPOSE THERE ARE SOME GAPS.
PERHAPS I CAN COME BACK TOMORROW AND FILL IT ALL IN.

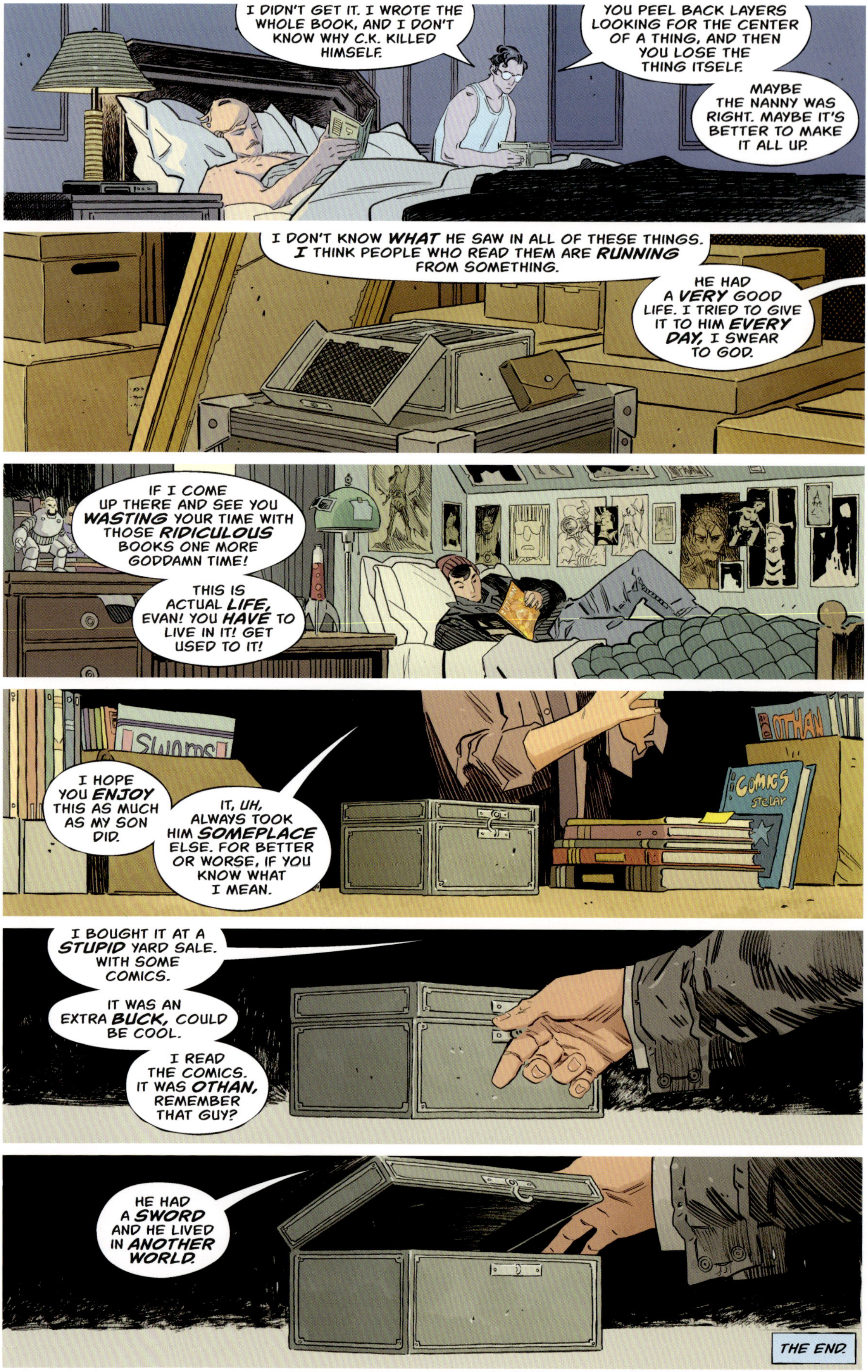
I DIDN'T GET IT. I WROTE THE WHOLE BOOK, AND I DON'T KNOW WHY C.K. KILLED HIMSELF.
YOU PEEL BACK LAYERS LOOKING FOR THE CENTER OF A THING, AND THEN YOU LOSE THE THING ITSELF.
MAYBE THE NANNY WAS RIGHT. MAYBE IT'S BETTER TO MAKE IT ALL UP.
I DON'T KNOW WHAT HE SAW IN ALL OF THESE THINGS. I THINK PEOPLE WHO READ THEM ARE RUNNING FROM SOMETHING.
HE HAD A VERY GOOD LIFE. I TRIED TO GIVE IT TO HIM EVERY DAY, I SWEAR TO GOD.
IF I COME UP THERE AND SEE YOU WASTING YOUR TIME WITH THOSE RIDICULOUS BOOKS ONE MORE GODDAMN TIME!
THIS IS ACTUAL LIFE, EVAN! YOU HAVE TO LIVE IN IT! GET USED TO IT!
I HOPE YOU ENJOY THIS AS MUCH AS MY SON DID.
IT, UH, ALWAYS TOOK HIM SOMEPLACE ELSE. FOR BETTER OR WORSE, IF YOU KNOW WHAT I MEAN.
COMICS
I BOUGHT IT AT A STUPID YARD SALE. WITH SOME COMICS.
IT WAS AN EXTRA BUCK, COULD BE COOL.
I READ THE COMICS. IT WAS OTHAN, REMEMBER THAT GUY?
HE HAD A SWORD AND HE LIVED IN ANOTHER WORLD.
THE END.

Helen of Wyndhorn #1 Cover C by **TULA LOTAY**

Helen of Wyndhorn #1 Cover D by **ELSA CHARRETIER**

Helen of Wyndhorn #1 Cover E by **MASSIMO CARNEVALE**

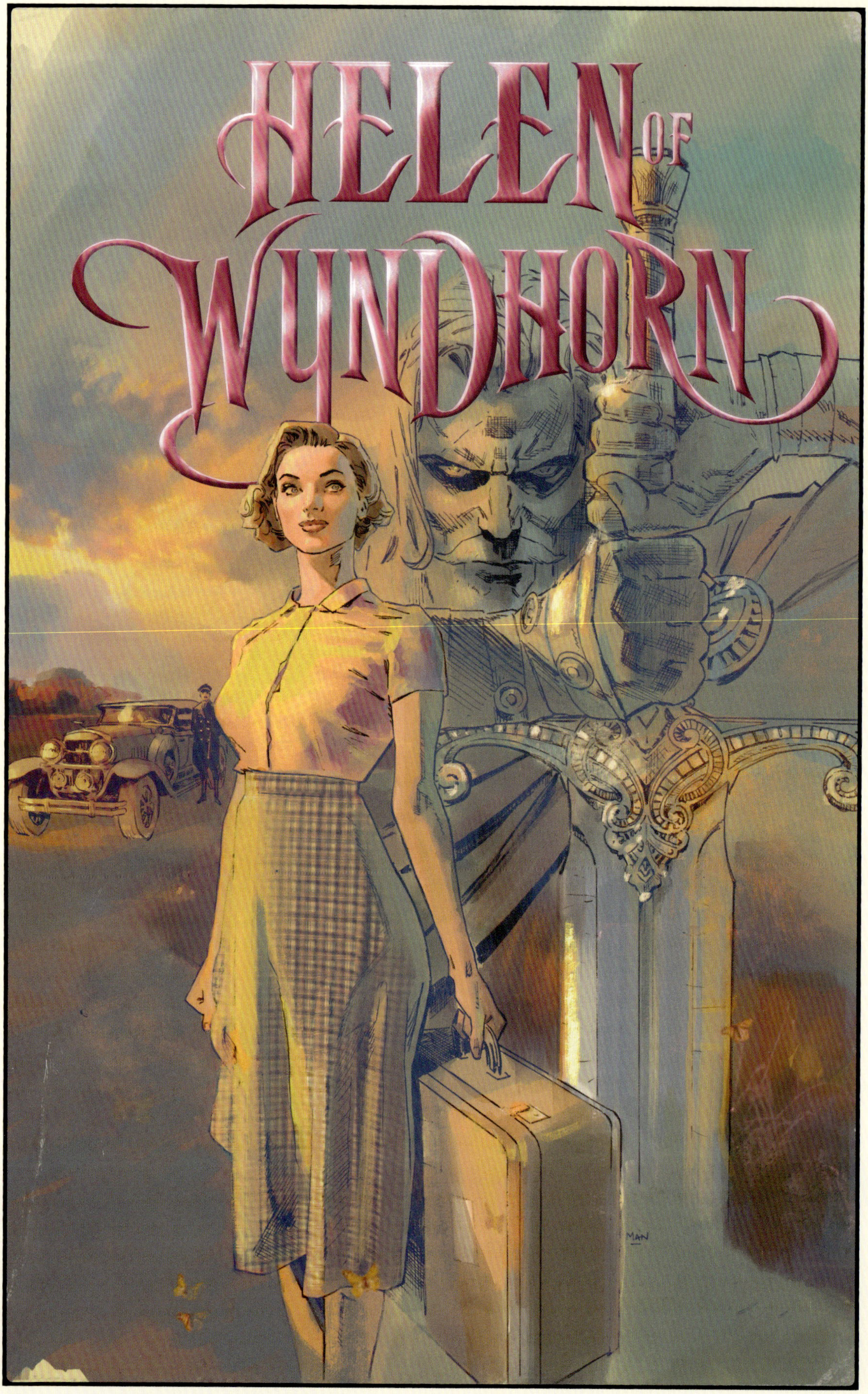

Helen of Wyndhorn #1 Cover F by **CLAY MANN**

Helen of Wyndhorn #1 Cover G by **WALT SIMONSON** with **LAURA MARTIN**

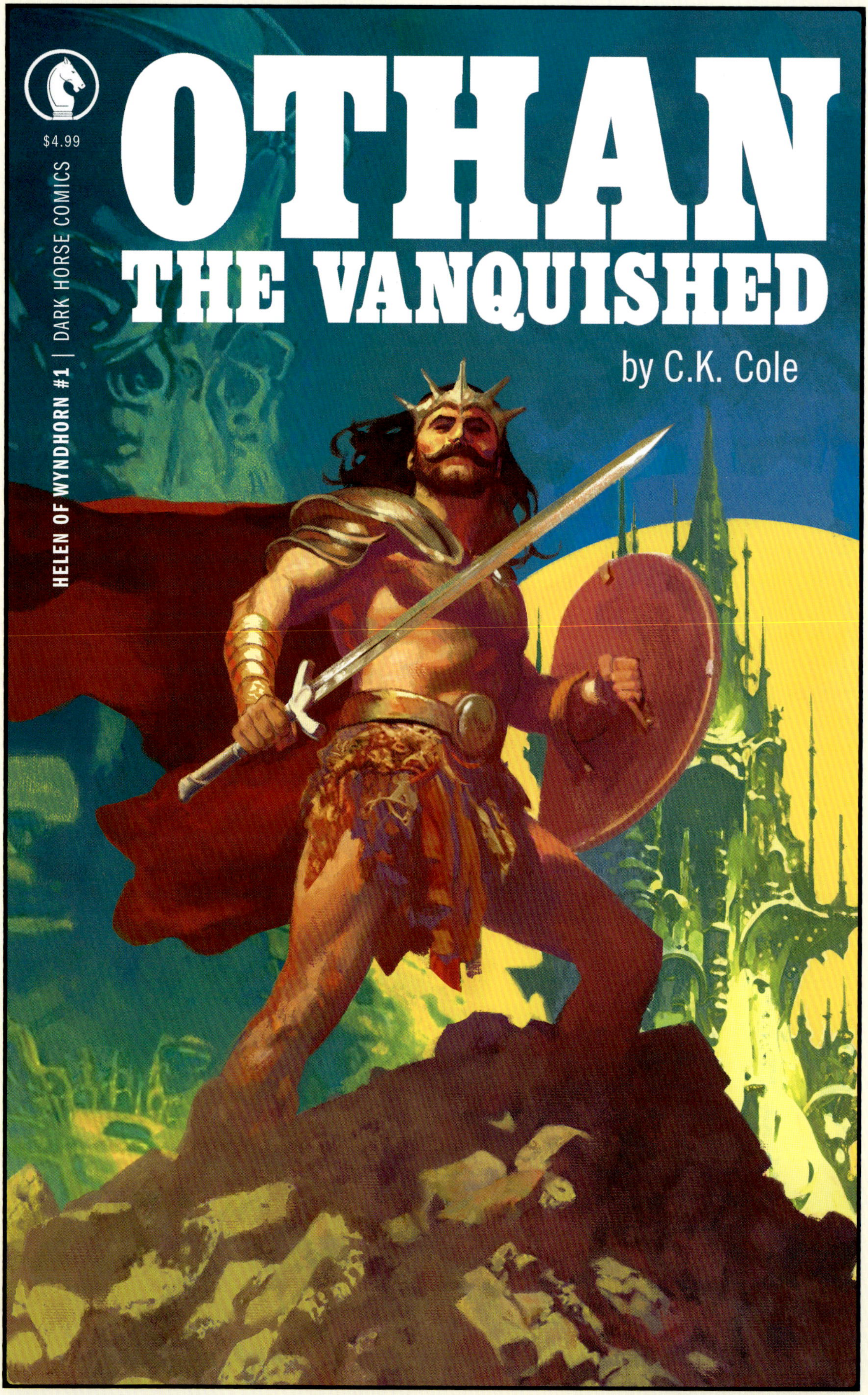

Helen of Wyndhorn #1 Cover H by **GREG SMALLWOOD**

Helen of Wyndhorn #2 Cover C by **GREG SMALLWOOD**

Helen of Wyndhorn #3 Cover C by **FÁBIO MOON**

Helen of Wyndhorn #4 Cover C by **JILL THOMPSON**

Helen of Wyndhorn #5 Cover C by **GABRIEL HERNÁNDEZ WALTA**

Helen of Wyndhorn #6 Cover C by **DAVID MACK**

SKETCHBOOK

Notes by **BILQUIS EVELY**

My initial focus in creating this new world was on Helen and Barnabas. It was more complex than expected because I could take many directions. I was meticulous about every detail in the book. It took me weeks to find the right hairstyle, eye format, height, and other aspects to ensure they were authentic and charismatic.

ESCADA MAIOR
ESPELHO
WATER?

Lilith and Joseph came to life quite quickly, which delighted me. This was a stark contrast to the challenges I faced with Wyndhorn. The house was the most difficult to conceptualize. After some time, I realized the house would be easier to depict on the pages rather than just in sketches. The same applied to the side characters, for whom I made preliminary concepts and let them grow in the pages where they appeared.

Helen of Wyndhorn is a book inspired by fantasy and Gothic romances. During the process, I researched several references to build a solid foundation for the characters and scenarios. These ranged from 1930s dresses and suits to warriors' armor and ancient swords, from Gothic mansions to romantic landscape art and fantasy atmosphere. The story features two distinct worlds with their own characteristics. What I love most is how both worlds complement each other, echoing a fantasy world inside a Gothic mansion and vice versa.

Before drawing a new comic book, I always deeply consider what art style I should seek. I found inspiration in old book and magazine illustrations, where I decided to focus on using delicate thin lines and black and white to create contrast.